Australia Travel Guide: Typical Costs & Money Tips, Sightseeing, Wilderness, Day Trips, Cuisine, Sydney, Melbourne, Brisbane, Perth, Adelaide, Newcastle, Canberra, Cairns and more

by Alex Pitt

Table of Contents

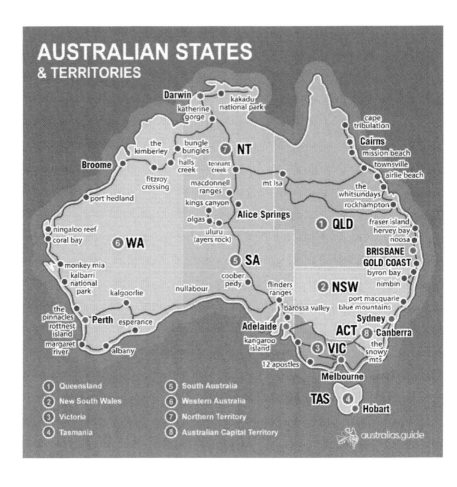

AUSTRALIAN STATES
& TERRITORIES

Darwin
kakadu
national park
katherine
gorge

the
kimberley
bungle
bungles
⑦ NT

Broome
halls
creek
tennant
creek

fitzroy
crossing
macdonnell
ranges
mt isa

port hedland
kings canyon

olgas
Alice Springs

ningaloo reef
coral bay
uluru
(ayers rock)

⑥ WA

monkey mia
kalbarri
national
park
kalgoorlie
nullabour
coober
pedy
flinders
ranges

⑤ SA

cape
tribulation

Cairns
mission beach
townsville
airlie beach

the
whitsundays
rockhampton

① QLD
fraser island
hervey bay
noosa

BRISBANE
GOLD COAST
byron bay
nimbin

② NSW
port macquarie
barossa valley
blue mountains

the
pinnacles
rottnest
island
Perth
esperance

margaret
river
albany

Adelaide
kangaroo
island

12 apostles

Sydney
ACT ⑧ Canberra
③ VIC
the
snowy
mts

Melbourne

TAS ④
Hobart

① Queensland	⑤ South Australia		
② New South Wales	⑥ Western Australia		
③ Victoria	⑦ Northern Territory		
④ Tasmania	⑧ Australian Capital Territory		

australias.guide

4

Introduction

Australia is a wild and beautiful place, a land whose color palette of red outback sands and Technicolor reefs frames sophisticated cities and soulful Indigenous stories.

Hip Cities

Most Australians live along the coast, and most of these folks live in cities – 89% of Australians, in fact. It follows that cities here are a lot of fun. Sydney is the glamorous poster child with world-class beaches and an otherwise glorious setting. Melbourne is all arts, alleyways and a stellar food scene. Brisbane is a subtropical town on the way up, Adelaide has festive grace and pubby poise. Boomtown Perth breathes West Coast optimism and Canberra showcases so many cultural treasures, while the tropical northern frontier town of Darwin, and the chilly southern sandstone city of Hobart, couldn't be more different.

Wild Lands & Wildlife

Australia is an extraordinarily beautiful place, as rich in rainforest (from Far North

Queensland to far-south Tasmania) as it is in remote rocky outcrops like Uluru, Kakadu and the Kimberleys. The coastline, too, beset as it is with islands and deserted shores, is wild and wonderful. Animating these splendid places is wildlife like nowhere else on the planet, a place of kangaroos and crocodiles, of wombats and wallabies, platypus, crocodiles, dingoes and so much more. Tracking these, and Australia's 700-plus bird species, is enough to unearth your inner David Attenborough, even if you didn't until now know you had one.

Epicurean Delights

Australia plates up a multicultural fusion of European techniques and fresh Pacific-rim ingredients – aka 'Mod Oz' (Modern Australian). Seafood plays a starring role – from succulent Moreton Bay bugs to delicate King George whiting. Of course, beer in hand, you'll still find beef, lamb and chicken at Aussie barbecues. Don't drink beer? Australian wines are world-beaters:

punchy Barossa Valley shiraz, Hunter Valley semillon and cool-climate Tasmanian sauvignon blanc. Tasmania produces outstanding whisky too. Need a caffeine hit? You'll find cafes everywhere, coffee machines in petrol stations, and baristas in downtown coffee carts.

The Open Road

There's a lot of tarmac across this wide brown land. From Margaret River to Cooktown, Jabiru to Dover, the best way to appreciate Australia is to hit the road. Car hire is relatively affordable, road conditions are generally good, and beyond the big cities traffic fades away. If you're driving a campervan, you'll find well-appointed caravan parks in most sizable towns. If you're feeling adventurous, hire a 4WD and go off-road: Australia's national parks and secluded corners are custom-made for camping trips down the dirt road and classic desert tracks from Birdsville to Cape York have adventure written all over them.

Australia is one of the most popular travel destinations in the world. It's known as a major backpacking, camping, road trip, and diving destination, but no matter your travel style, there is something to draw you here. The country is filled with incredible natural beauty from Uluru to the Outback, rainforests to pristine white sand beaches, and of course, the Great Barrier Reef. Sydney's Harbor Bridge and Opera House are iconic man-made wonders, and Melbourne's café culture will make you feel like you are in Europe. Coupled with world-class surfing, and it is no wonder people never leave. I've been over five times and have crisscrossed it three time but, every trip, I find something new about this country to love. Use my extensive travel guide to help plan your next trip. I know you will love the country as much as I do!

Typical Costs

Accommodation – Hostels start at 20 AUD per night for a dorm room, though they get as high as 40 in the big coastal cities. Private rooms with a double bed and a shared bathroom in hostels range between 80-100 AUD per night. For budget hotels, you are looking to spend at least around 75-95 AUD for a double room, private bathroom, TV, and breakfast. Larger, chain hotels cost closer to 200 AUD. Camping costs between 15-30 AUD per night (cheaper if you bring your own tent, more expensive if you're parking an RV). Read more: My favorite hostels in Australia.

Food – Food isn't cheap in Australia! Most decent restaurant entrees cost at least 20 AUD. Originally, I thought I was doing something wrong spending so much, but as many of my Aussie friends told me, "we just get screwed here." If you cook your meals, expect to pay 100 AUD per week for groceries that will include pasta, vegetables, chicken, and other basic foodstuffs. Grab and go places cost around 8-10 AUD for sandwiches. Fast food is around 15 AUD for a meal (burger, fries, soda). The best value food are the Asian and Indian restaurants where you can get a really filling meal for under $10 AUD!

Transportation – Local city trains and buses cost 3-4 AUD. The easiest way to get around the country is via Greyhound. Passes begin at 145 AUD and go all the way to 3,000 AUD. There are also backpacker buses like the Oz Experience that have multi-city passes starting at 535 AUD (though I don't like the Oz Experience and wouldn't recommend it). The most popular and cheapest way to travel is to drive yourself. Campervan rentals start at 60 AUD per day and can also double as places to sleep. Flying can be very expensive due to limited competition, especially when going from coast to coast. I generally avoid flying in Australia unless I am pressed for time or there is a sale.

Activities – Multi-day activities and tours are expensive, generally costing 400-540 AUD. Day trips will cost about 135-230 AUD. For example, a one-day trip to the Great Barrier Reef can cost 230 AUD while a two-night sailing trip around the Whitsunday Islands can cost upwards of 540 AUD. A three-day trip to Uluru from Alice Springs is around 480 AUD. Walking tours are around 50 AUD and day trips to wine regions are between 150-200 AUD.

Suggested daily budget

$60-80 AUD / 43-57 USD (Note: This is a suggested budget assuming you're staying in a hostel, eating out a little, cooking most of your meals, and using local transportation. This also depends greatly on the number of tours you do! Using the budget tips below, you can always lower this number. However, if you stay in fancier accommodation or eat out more often, expect this to be higher!)

Money Saving Tips

Get a phone plan – The telephone company Telstra has really improved their service and offers great phone packages that have great coverage throughout the country. Their call/text rates aren't that high either, so the credit will last you awhile. Vodafone has amazing deals (sometimes better) too but they have more limited coverage around the country.

Drink goon (box wine) – Goon is infamous on the Australian backpacker hostel trail. This cheap box of wine is the best way to drink, get a buzz, and save a lot of money at the same time. 4 liters typically costs 13 AUD (compared to a six pack of beer for the same Price). Drink this before you go out and save on spending money at the bar (where it is about 10 AUD per drink).

Cook often – Again, eating out is not cheap. The best way to reduce your costs is to cook as many meals as possible. ALDI is the cheapest supermarket in the country, followed by Coles and then Woolworths (though sometimes you don't get a choice at which place you can shop it! Some small towns only have one!).

Car share – Australia is a big country that can be expensive to get around. If you are traveling with friends, it's smart to buy a used car or campervan (or rent a new one from one of the many rental companies in the country) and split the costs of gas. You can also hitch a ride with other travelers using sites like Gumtree, Jayride, or a hostel message board.

Book tours as a package – This country has a lot of exciting activities and tours that eat into any budget. Booking activities together through a hostel or tour agency will get you a discount and save you hundreds of dollars as a repeat customer.

Seek out free Internet – The internet in Australia is painfully slow and expensive (just ask any Australian how they feel about this), but libraries and McDonalds have free WiFi that you can use.

Work for your room – Many hostels offer travelers the opportunity to work for their accommodation. In exchange for a few hours a day of cleaning, you get a free bed to sleep in. Commitments vary but most hostels ask that you stay for at least a week.

WWOOF it! – WWOOFing is a program that allows you to work on organic farms in exchange for free room and board. Everyone I've met who stays in the country long term does it for at least one month. You don't even need to know anything about farming – you're mostly picking fruit the whole time! It's a great way to reduce your expenses and make an impact on the local environment.

Couchsurf – Accommodation in Australia can be quite Pricey. If you plan ahead, you can usually find really nice Couchsurfing hosts all throughout the country. This way, you not only have a place to stay but you'll have a local host that can tell you the best places to go and things to see.

Fill up your water bottle – The tap water is clean and safe to drink in Australia. Cutting the 2-3 AUD for each bottle of water will reduce your daily spending. Not buying bottles of water also good environmental impact too!

Sightseeing in Canberra: discover essential landmarks in the Aussie capital

The capital city of Canberra today is a living embodiment of the nation's quickly evolving arts, architecture and cultural scenes. It's just over a hundred years old, and this relative youth gives it a unique kind of energy. Canberra's chief architect crowed to the New York Times in 1913, "I have planned a city not like any other city in the world." And he was right.

This former sheep pasture halfway between rival cities Sydney and Melbourne stands among grand urban designs like Washington D.C. as a purpose-built and painstakingly designed environment. The city also boasts a burgeoning batch of top-notch dining, from the delectable sashimi and oysters at Akiba to the utterly unique take on modern-Australian at Aubergine. Fueling up visitors on foodie fare and the city's innovative design, Canberra is a town that makes good old-fashioned sightseeing a lot of fun.

Rich art and culture adventures

On the breezy Acton Peninsula, you'll find the strikingly post-modern design of the National Museum of Australia. The museum's most visible trait is its looping, sculptural architecture that curls over peaceful Lake Burley Griffin (elements allude to Australia's famous Uluru) and extends a pathway into the museum. The museum itself is a storehouse of Australian culture, with exhibits on Indigenous artifacts and art to an enormous reconstructed local dinosaur – the Muttaburrasaurus – and one of Australia's most iconic cars.

You'll find even more cultural gems when you cross over to the southern side of the lake. Before you even get across the bridge, you'll spot the iconic columns of the National Library of Australia. Hit the Library to explore a treasure trove of archival objects from the journal of Captain Cook to torches from Australia's Olympics in Melbourne and Sydney.

Walking up Reconciliation Place from the Library leads you past the National Portrait Gallery before concluding at the National Gallery of Australia. The Gallery has an embarrassment of aesthetic riches featuring Monet, Warhol and Salvador Dali's whimsical 'Lobster Telephone'. The Gallery also boasts the world's largest collection of Aboriginal and Torres Strait Islander artworks including The Aboriginal Memorial, a stunning display of 200 hollow log coffins from 43 Aboriginal artists representing 200 years of European occupation of Australia. Outside, you'll find the Sculpture Garden, including Fujiko Nakaya's eerie 'fog sculpture', which visitors experience by walking through wooded paths past a marsh pond enshrouded in floating banks of fog.

The Australian War Memorial

A visit to the Australian War Memorial is always worth the effort. The building itself is a beauty – a sandstone building close to the sprawling Mount Ainslie Nature Reserve that's crowned by a dome of burnished copper, built to epic scale to memorialize soldiers who fought in World War I. Since its construction, it's come to memorialize soldiers in all conflicts in which the Australian military has been involved

The war holds special significance here since, as a newly minted nation in 1901, World War I came to Australia as a chance to earn its stripes on a global stage.

Thousands of Australians enlisted (and many gave their lives).

Visitors to the site's Hall of Memory have admired saint-like mosaics of the fallen from World War II. The memorial's Anzac Hall (with an immersive night bombing raid experience) and Roll of Honour (where Australia's lost soldiers are honored every day at 4:55pm in the Last Post Ceremony) are also essential visits.

Historic seats of power

Australia's elegant Old Parliament House serves nowadays as the Museum of Australian Democracy (MOAD). It's an interesting place to experience - from 1927 to 1988, it served as the seat of government. Walking the halls of this historic building, you'll still feel the remaining parliamentary tension as you check out ornate bells mounted in every room, which once rang to summon Parliamentarians to vote. Even bathrooms were not exempt from bells ringing to call for an urgent vote. Elegant though it is, the building was only ever seen as temporary and was designed to last only 50 years.

Going back even farther than the Old Parliament House, Aboriginal and Torres Strait Islanders lived here long before Europeans bumped onto the continent. So you may be interested in visiting the Aboriginal Tent Embassy, the site of an ongoing encampment started in 1972 by four Aboriginal men to ask for land rights and preservation of sacred sites across the nation. Today you'll know it by a series of tents and encampments and a fire lit to mark ownership of the land.

Modern Parliament

By 1988 when Parliament moved uphill to dominate the skyline from Capital Hill, the building was straining to hold a growing government. So when it came to the new Parliament House, they upsized everything, and it's a sight to behold. There are over 4000 rooms in this huge, modernist structure. Even the iconic flag post is crafted from shining steel, weighing 250 tons. It's held up by four structures reminiscent of two clashing boomerangs.

Inside, the members of Australia's two houses of government – the House of Representatives and the Senate – meet in their red and green chambers. You can catch an often-spirited parliamentary debate here depending on the calendar. From Parliament House, you can also get a great perspective on the city's top-level design: look down the hill to see MOAD align with Australian War Memorial for a stunning realization of Burley Griffin's vision.

Exploring the wild world of Canberra's unexpected outdoor activities

If you think of Australia's capital as just another seat of government, you need to get outdoors more. Canberrans are an active crowd, savoring the weekend to hike, bike or ski away a working week in their backyard. The Australian Capital Territory boasts adrenaline-charged downhill cycling, hiking to Aboriginal rock art sites and plenty of chances to encounter unique fauna in its natural environment. So loosen the tie, grab some hiking boots and get set to make the most of the city known as the 'Bush Capital'.

Best biking

Weaving through its leafy environs, Canberra's excellent bike paths make it possible to wheel through much of the city. To get into gear, pedal around Lake Burley

Griffin, designed as Canberra's centerpiece and when the sun glitters across the water you can see why it's the dazzling heart of the city. It's popular with weekend walkers and lunchtime runners, but you can cover more ground cycling. The easiest ride is the central loop that takes in some of the city's most significant monuments. It can be spectacular when the Captain Cook Memorial Jet is firing jets of water into the spring sunshine.

A favorite lake ride is the Western Loop taking in the National Museum of Australia, skirting through the woods out to Scrivener Dam then past the elephant trumpets of the National Zoo and Aquarium and round past Yarralumla. Allow two hours so you can stop off to enjoy views up to the Arboretum or just catch your breath (there are a couple of hills but nothing major). The Eastern Loop gets a little wilder out through the Jerrabomberra Wetlands though you can stop for a civilized coffee at the Old Bus Depot Markets. All of these routes are well signposted plus there's a handy map online so you can link the routes into a day's cycling.

For a longer ride, the Centenary Trail makes for a three-day cycle, taking in much of Canberra. If you're after more rugged terrain, Stromlo Forest Park has excellent mountain biking, including bouncing over the 2km Vapour Trail, a series of jumps that gets more intense the further you go.

Adventures on foot

While it's a great bike ride, taking the Centenary Trail at hiking pace makes for a solid week of walking that lets you enjoy the terrain and wildlife along the way. Kicking off at Parliament House, the 145km trail wends in and out of the city and all throughout the ACT. It takes in Mount Stromlo, the iconic Black Mountain and the historic town of Hall. If you haven't got seven days to do the whole trail, bite off a shorter section like 8km legstretcher from Kambah Pool to Tuggeranong Town Centre.

Further afield, Namadgi National Park promises more hardcore bushwalking (Australian for hiking) through eerie granite boulders, huts and homes from Australia's colonial history and further back to see Aboriginal rock art. One of the easiest strolls is the 6km Yankee Hat Track that takes you to Canberra's only known rock art by the Ngunnawal people who painted clay and ochre interpretations of humans and animals to puzzle over. Check in at the visitors centre to find a walk that suits and ensure the right trail conditions before heading out.

Pick up the pace with a run around Lake Burley Griffin by following the lakeside loops. In April, the Australian Running Festival takes to the streets with a full marathon or shorter 5km jogs – which all take in the lake and Parliament House.

Wildlife spotting

There are plenty of chances to spot wildlife throughout the Bush Capital. It's hard to miss kangaroos bouncing around Mount Ainslie or Mount Majura with dusk the best time to watch the marsupials slowly grazing on the slopes. But Tidbinbilla is your best bet to check off Australia's unique fauna in its habitat. Not far from the Tidbinbilla visitors centre, you'll spot roos and mobs of emus pecking their way around grasslands.

If you venture just a little further into the park, there's a koala sanctuary that makes one of the best places to meet the furry critters as they are well protected and consequently are among the nation's cheeriest bears. Take the short Sanctuary Loop to have potaroos scampering across your trail and you might even spot a reclusive echidna trundling off to hoover up ants. For a unique furry friend, you can search out the platypus in Black Flats Dam. They're known for having stage fright if you're in a larger and noisier group, but with a quiet approach you might spy the duck-billed divas scurrying into water for a paddle.

Winter wanderlust

In winter, Canberra gets gentle snowfalls that you can spot when the nearby Brindabella Ranges put on their winter coat. If you've got the room in the itinerary, a few days in the Snowy Mountains (affectionately called the Snowies by most locals) make for atmospheric skiing through gum trees with runs to suit most levels of experience.

But if you're just keen for some snowplay and beginners skiing, Corin Forest gives a taste of the snow within an hour's drive of the city. Half-day ski classes are perfect starters for junior snow bunnies. If all that falling down proves too much for kids there's always a snowball fight and all will be forgiven for a hot chocolate around the impressive indoor fire.

Wet and wild

When the snows start to melt, Canberra's surrounding waterways become a playground for rafting, kayaking and stand up paddleboarding. The Murrumbidgee and Snowy rivers both rush with white water that makes for brilliant rafting. Unless you bring your own gear, it's easiest to partner with local operators such as Alpine River Adventures who do 1-2 day trips and know their way down the best (and worst) rapids.

For something a little tamer there's plenty of good swimming holes around the capital. Taking to the lake in a kayak is an effortless way to see the capital and you can hire from YMCA's Paddle Hub. For swimming, try Kambah Pool, your chance to swim in a gum tree-lined gorge amid cockatoo squawks on thc Murrumbidgee River. There are sandy beaches that make for perfect picnicking as well as a dedicated nudist area around the bend.

Only in Canberra

Exhausted yet? Save some energy for an experience that you can only have in the capital. Sure, cycling past the Parliament is fine or spotting kangaroos minutes from a city centre is impressive, but top it all by looking down on Canberra from a balloon to witness the whole city set amid bushland. The best time to hit the heights is during the

Canberra Balloon Spectacular in March, held on the lawns of Old Parliament House, a venue that has created more than its fair share of hot air. The festival offers balloons of all shapes – in the past there have been Angry Birds, Yoda and Smurfs gazing down contentedly at the capital. Outside of the festival, Balloons Aloft and Dawn Drifters offer the best perspective of Canberra and its wild surrounds. Both the city and its wilderness will reward the adventurous.

10 ways the Gold Coast will surprise you

There's more to this glitzy beach-side city than high-rises and rollers! The Gold Coast has a wealth of natural geographical beauty, healthy haunts and curious culture to offer alongside the mega-clubs and super yachts. Once you start to delve a little deeper, you could be pleasantly surprised by the many quirks and intricacies flying under the radar at this notorious holiday hot spot.

The green behind the gold

Weaving through the concrete jungle of Surfers Paradise, you'd never guess that a World Heritage-listed wilderness is less than an hour's drive away. Springbrook and Lamington National Parks make a refreshing escape from the city bustle, and offer spectacular bush walks through historical rainforests. Start with the rewarding Purling Brook Falls circuit in Springbrook and cap it off with scenic eye candy at the aptly named Best of All Lookout just down the road.

Secret swimming holes

The beaches here are already legendary, but they're not the only place to take a dip. The Gold Coast is peppered with magnificent waterfalls and natural swimming holes that offer cool respite from the sizzling sand and powerful surf. One of the best has to be Cougal Cascades at the edge of Springbrook National Park, where you can marinate in a series of pretty, terraced pools formed over thousands of years of natural water erosion.

Edible enjoyment

The GC has never been renowned for subtlety – this is a city where gold bikini-clad 'meter maids' were once the star attraction, after all – but the famously flashy town is fast developing cool-kid cred. Photogenic cafes and restaurants are popping up all along the coast: at Burleigh Heads, the achingly hip Rick Shores restaurant teams smart pan-Asian fare with a show-stopping view. Meanwhile in Mermaid Beach, Bam Bam Bakehouse combines a rustic French fit-out with truly drool-worthy pastries.

Serious shopping

A jaw-dropping $670 million expansion has transformed the tired Pacific Fair mall at Broadwater into a fashionista's dream. With flagship stores from the world's top labels and a luxe tropical vibe, it's less like a shopping centre and feels more akin to visiting a resort. If you're not keen on tackling the mega complex, go treasure hunting in the Gold Coast's back streets instead. You can find the signature peach door of garden-slash-homeware store The Borrowed Nursery nestled between warehouses and garages in Mermaid Beach, and an enclave of fashion boutiques championing Aussie labels on James Street in Burleigh Heads.

Totally wild locals

The lush coastline is home to an array of wildlife, from koalas and kangaroos to a staggering range of native and migratory birds. You don't even have to leave the city to catch a glimpse: Federation Walk near Main Beach is a relaxing 3km stroll through a diverse bird habitat. Keep your eyes peeled for the colourful rainbow bee-eater and the striking red-backed fairywren as you meander through dunes and coastal forest.

A vibrant arts scene

With its dazzling casinos and bedazzled locals you could be forgiven for thinking the Goldie is somewhat lacking in substance, but there's a thriving arts scene harboured amidst the glitz for culture-vultures to explore. The trick is to look where you least expect it, like in an industrial zone just behind Mermaid Beach. That's where you'll find 19 Karen, a sprawling art space filled with work from local and international contemporary artists. If you take your art with a side of espresso, head to Dust Temple in Currumbin Waters, a cool creative space that's both gallery and café.

Home grown glitter

Linger in the rainforest after dark and you'll realise this area has always been organically adorned with bling. Australia's largest colony of glow worms create a magical fairyland under Natural Bridge in Springbrook National Park, while glowing fireflies and luminescent fungi light up seasonally throughout the national parks for nocturnal explorers with a keen eye.

Bars with personality

This city isn't immune to the secret bar trend, and its bustling highway is the perfect spot to hide tiny, trendy speakeasies. If you can drag yourself away from the glamorous water views of the tourist traps, you'll find an exciting world of underground drinking dens. In Broadwater, a door masquerading as telephone box marks the entrance to Soho Place, a nook serving high-end cocktails. Then there's the appropriately named Hidden, in Tugun, dishes up tapas and wine to accompany live music and burlesque, of course.

Farm-fresh goodness

Thanks to its lush hinterland and tropical weather, the Gold Coast is blessed with amazing fresh produce. You can quite literally get your hands on it at biodynamic farm Currumbin Valley Harvest. Open on weekends only, the unique site allows visitors to pick their own produce from the abundant veggie patch, stock up on more local farm-fresh supplies in the shop, and finish off with a cuppa in the creek-side café.

Coastal serenity

Think it's all about the bright lights of a big city on a busy beach? This isn't Miami, but Australia, where laid-back living is an art form. Take a turn off the hectic Gold Coast Highway at Tallebudgera Creek and you'll find yourself in a peaceful paradise where the calm river laps a sandy, palm-fringed shore – perfect for a lazy stand up paddle or swim. There are many more pockets of tranquility all along this 57km stretch of coastline – why not make it your mission to find a favorite.

A secret-spots guide to Perth's hip neighbourhoods

A cluster of urban villages surrounds the heart of Perth city. Each has its own distinctive personality, whether hipster, grungy, multicultural or trendy, turning an exploration of each into a fun observation of Western Australian society. These buzzing neighbourhoods are also where a bunch of the best restaurants, bars and boutiques are, each reflecting their locale's defining style.

Hipster heaven: Leederville

Leederville is having a moment. Its eclectic strip brims with people sipping coffee or wine in the sunshine from 10am (when cafes, restaurants and shops open) until late into the night. Most stores don't close until 10pm and its nightlife, naturally, kicks on much later. The train ride is a mere three minutes from the city.

From the exit, pop out at Oxford St and turn left into Kailis Fish Market, which gives a good insight into local seafood such as marron and rock lobster. If you're on a tight budget, Siena's does cheap pasta and pizza, but spend a smidge more and have a tastier experience across the road at Spanish tapas house Pinchos.

Opposite Pinchos, Bill's Bar and Bites gets energetic on weekends, while Foam, back on Oxford St, has pavement-facing couches made for people watching. Leederville has free wifi (look for the City of Vincent Network) and freelancers often work from Foam's big inside table. For shopping, local shoe store Hunter is hard to beat, ditto Varga

Girl (best be cashed up). Moving away from the main strip, there are some hideaway stars. Kitsch has excellent mod-Asian in upcycled surrounds; next door Italian alimenteri the Re Store does the best continental rolls in town, and across the road, Pixel Coffee Brewers gets high-fives for its brews and breakfasts.

Multicultural mish-mash: Northbridge

This is the city centre's gritty little delinquent sister. Divided from the shinier city zone for the past century (and due to be reunited early in 2018 by a huge pedestrian zone), Northbridge has evolved into a hotbed of cultures. Waves of Chinese, Italian, Greek, Indian and Vietnamese migrants have arrived in the West, bringing cheap and cheerful restaurants to the concrete and neon landscape. New Moon does excellent all-day dim sum, Viet Hoa aces steaming pho, Lucky Chan's specialises in ramen and a funky rooftop and, for something upmarket, Shadow's sexy interiors give way to sharp modern

European fare. Start your Northbridge immersion with a wander along William St, where you'll find home grown designers (I love Merge, run by a WA fashion graduate, Periscope for its upmarket tailoring and Fi and Co for whimsical, vintage pieces) and, up the far end, a brilliant edit of unusual gifts at William Topp.

If you're starting later in the day, head upstairs to Mechanics Institute rooftop bar – it's accessed via a narrow laneway leading off the Perth Cultural Centre. Kick on to Sneaky Tony's (get the password from its Facebook page), swing back to The Bird for a hit of live music then on to Ezra Pound for grungy cocktails. Finish off at a dive bar with a rocking, after-midnight dancefloor, Joe's Juice Joint. Two other little secrets for you: ChiCho Gelato does the finest handmade gelato this side of the Nullarbor and Rooftop Movies is an open air cinema on top of a car park – go when it's showing golden oldies. Bonus tip: Alex Hotel is the coolest and best located accommodation in the city.

Stylish and smooth: Subiaco

One of Perth's 'leafy' suburbs, its residential areas are split by a cross shape, cut by Hay St and Rockeby Rd. There's plenty on each, from cafes to boutiques, bars and big, beer-focused pubs. One of its quirks is a cat café named Purrth. You can book in for 30 or 60 minute sessions with the resident rescue cats (and yes Purrth cat cafe has an animal welfare policy, we asked). Another magnetic force is the Saturday Subiaco Farmers Market. From 8am to 12 noon, you can fill your hessian shopping tote with local fruit and veg, crusty bread, instagram-worthy cupcakes and cured meats.

While much of 'Subi' has an up market-meets-commercial feel, if you head south on Rockeby to the Kings Park end, you'll find a cluster of gems. On the corner of Heytesbury Rd, Juanita's bar is a local's haunt that spills onto the pavement. A bit tiki, a bit upcycled and a lot of fun, it has a well curated wine list and excellent mezze platters (the owner's artworks grace the walls). A couple doors down, Lady of Ro does char grilled Mediterranean dinners by candelight. Then there's Boucla Kafenion, a chaotically busy cafe with a Moroccan den vibe. I've been drinking great coffee and inhaling even greater cakes here for years.

For foodies, Subiaco has two standouts: Lulu la Delizia, for handmade pasta using recipes from Italy's Friuli region (pinched from the chef's nonna) and New Normal, a slick modern eatery where vegetable dishes often give their meaty equivalents a run for their money. Both venues are off Subiaco's well beaten main drags.

Byron Bay's best day trips

If you've managed to get your fill of Byron Bay's legendary beaches, it's time to switch it up and explore your surroundings with a day trip. Take the scenic route out of Byron (as the locals call it) to discover the region's quaint villages, cool culinary delights, hippy enclaves and, okay, maybe a few more beaches…

Village life in Mullumbimby

The region's alternative spirit is alive and thriving in Mullumbimby, a small but vibrant village at the foot of Mount

Chincogan. To get there, take Ewingsdale Road out of Byron Bay – stopping for a tour and some sustainable snacks at The Farm. Then swing onto Coolamon Scenic Drive, a winding country trail that offers sweeping views across rolling hills to the cape. Along the way you'll pass Crystal Castle, a unique attraction where you can wander a labyrinth and commune with the tallest crystals in the world.

Time your trip to Mullumbimby for a Friday morning to experience the town's bustling farmer's market from 7am to 11am. Mullum's leafy showground bursts with stalls selling organic produce, flowers and tempting breakfasts, while locals catch up over coffee. Later, stroll the palm-lined main street and stock up on fresh sourdough at Scratch Patisserie, sink a schooner at the grand Middle Pub or indulge at the lush Kiva Spa.

Food and fossicking in Brunswick Heads

Just north of Byron Bay lies the sleepy holiday village of Brunswick Heads, a little smaller than its counterpart down the road but just as charming. If you're visiting Mullumbimby, it's just a short detour east, otherwise head north on the freeway from Byron. Bruns (yes, locals do love shortening names) is a vintage shopper's dream. Driving into town you'll pass sprawling antique stores like Clem's Cargo and A Curious Collective, while the streets closer to the river are peppered with shops stuffed with secondhand treasures and handcrafted homewares.

Brunswick's idyllic river and beach combo might be the main allure for holidaymakers, but its excellent food fare is just one more attractive reason to stick around. Leading the charge is Fleet, a sliver of a restaurant with a reputation that belies its size: book well in advance to experience the sophisticated seasonal menu. A few steps away, Milk Bar is reinventing the Aussie corner shop concept, serving up spicy bibimbap bowls and tacos along with coffee and ice cream. And if you're a fan of lazy Sundays, get down to the recently revamped

Brunswick Picture House and enjoy your breakfast accompanied by live music in their funky retro garden.

Rewind time in Newrybar and Bangalow

An easy day trip for first-timers to Byron, these pint-sized towns offer big rewards. Head south from Byron and turn right onto Midgen Flat Road at Broken Head for a charming country drive dotted with roadside farm stalls and you'll emerge opposite the historic village of Newrybar on Hinterland Way. Established in 1881 it's now a blink-and-you'll-miss-it strip of boutique goodness. Start with coffee and a fresh pastry from acclaimed restaurant Harvest's deli, then wander around the organic kitchen garden below. Across the road you'll find Newrybar Merchants, a bower-like co-op where local creatives display their wares, from pottery to luxe, one-of-a-kind bed linen.

A five-minute cruise down Hinterland Way should land you in Bangalow, once known for its dairy farms and now home to a cluster of chic boutiques, like the achingly cool Island Luxe, as well as a handful of upmarket cafes, a well-preserved 1940s pub and an art deco patisserie. Keep an eye out for plaques detailing the town's intriguing history as you tour the streets.

Surf and turf in Lennox Head

Visitors flying into the Ballina Byron Airport are likely to catch a glimpse of majestic Lennox Head on their way to Byron Bay. It's worth taking a 15-minute drive back to explore this relaxed surf strip. Take the Coast Road south from Byron for a highlight reel of Northern Rivers scenery: you'll pass through picturesque pockets of subtropical vegetation, cane fields and a forest of tea trees before turning into Lennox Head.

Experienced surfers will be frothing for the powerful right-hand point break below the headland, but you won't miss out if hanging ten's not your thing. Potter along the path over the headland for dramatic views of the coastline, or head down to Seven Mile

Beach for an ocean swim before dipping into the cool, fresh water of Lake Ainsworth, just behind the beach a little north of town.

Finish your day trip with an Aussie tradition: takeaway fish and chips on the grass overlooking the beach, followed by a scoop of your favorite flavour from the indulgent Lennox Gelato & Coffee Co.

Good vibes in Nimbin

The heartland of Northern Rivers counter culture, Nimbin morphed from a sleepy farming town to the nation's hippy capital in 1973, after hosting the Aquarius Festival – Australia's version of Woodstock. Forty years on, it remains a psychedelic homage to alternative lifestyles. Located 70km west of Byron Bay, the trip to Nimbin is a dreamy tour of lush hinterland and rainforest. Plan your visit for the second Sunday of the month and you'll run into a huge craft market at The Channon, a small village on the edge of Nightcap National Park.

Continue on to Nimbin and stroll the colourful main strip: soak up the street art, visit the Hemp Embassy and explore the quirky galleries and shops before stopping for wood-fired pizza at Nimbin Pizza & Trattoria. Nimbin is surrounded by natural wonders, including Nimbin Rocks, three rhyolite extrusions created by a volcanic eruption 20 million years ago. A significant cultural site for the local Bundjalung people, it's best viewed from a lookout 2km out of town.

Sun, snacks and shopping: explore Sydney's outdoor markets

If you want to sway to Sydney's song, visit its free outdoor markets where the local rhythm is relaxed and lingers all afternoon. Sure, you might grab a bargain, but the markets are also an excuse to slip out for some sunshine, catch up on the gossip, eat too much and show off a summer outfit!

The Rocks Weekend Market

Why here: The Rocks Markets are nestled among some of Sydney's most recognisable postcard monuments: the Sydney Harbour Bridge and Opera House. The Rocks are where modern Sydney first settled and the market spreads between cobblestone streets and elegant warehouses, conveniently blending into adjacent bars, pubs, restaurants, boutique wool stores, the Museum of Contemporary Art and that stunning harbour.

Best buys: Designer clothes, home-wares and hats are more common here than a bargain. Look for crafty souvenirs such as hanging ornaments made from bits of Australian trees, and hand-carved chopping blocks that still smell of eucalyptus. Cool down with traditional lemonade.

When: 10am-5pm, Saturday & Sunday. The Rocks Foodie Market is on 9am-3pm, Fridays, yum.

Bondi Markets

Why here: Bondi beach is just across the road, so you can smell the surf and sunscreen while perusing Bondi Markets. The dress code is beachcomber casual and the stalls are placed within Bondi Beach Public School with a functioning canteen for food and drink, giving you the chance to relive your school heydays.

Best buys: Objects to take you back to a slower era such as retro home-wares, antiques, vintage clothes and essential oils. The Farmer's Market has organic and vegetarian food, eco products and boutique food trucks.

When: 10am-4pm, Sunday. Farmer's Market 9am-1pm on Saturdays.

Newtown Market

Why here: Newton Market is both cool and tiny, and although there isn't much to grab you for longer than half an hour, it's worth visiting to get the full hit of the town's alternative chic all in one spot. Barefoot locals in shorts and young designer-label-clad couples alike browse the market on their way to the park or airy cafes. Buskers and street poets add to Newtown's artsy, activist reputation. There are no food stalls but it's on the same street as ample Thai restaurants and places to grab a gourmet pie, taco or gelato.

Best buys: Old vinyl, and well-polished, if gimmicky, crafts by local artisans. Think wine bottles made into plant holders that you might actually want.

When: 10am-4pm, Saturday.

Glebe Markets

Why here: Where Sydneysiders go to browse, sit, relax and people-watch. The Glebe Markets are set in a large school playground, where big kids can lounge about with satay sticks, macaroons and other food truck treats. There's typically some live music on the go (nothing too rowdy) for a hint of that festival vibe. With Sydney University and cheap hostels around the corner, come here to mix with students and travellers in a chilled-out vibe.

Best buys: Trash and treasure. Vintage clothing bargains, second-hand books, vinyl, handcrafted designs and antiques.

When: 10am-4pm, Saturday. Come early for the good stuff or late for bargains from tired first-time sellers who don't want to have to take anything home.

Rozelle Collectors Markets

Why here: Hardly a tourist in sight and nobody is in a rush at the varied outdoor Rozelle Collectors Market. Many stalls are run by groups of young friends who live locally and are doing it more for the experience than making a living. There are plenty of bargains, especially for vintage clothes and bric-a-brac.

Best buys: Preloved designer and brand clothing from the 90s onwards. There are stalls brandishing collectibles from Barbie dolls and crockery to ornate vintage kimonos.

When: 9am-3pm, Saturday & Sunday.

Marrickville Organic Food and Farmers' Markets

Why here: Marrickville is the go-to suburb now that Newtown's surging rents have pushed out some of the locals. The Organic Food and Farmers Market is bursting with color – with fresh fruit and veg, crystals, teas and plants spilling out of the stalls. Pay a visit to Reverse Garbage while you're here – a fascinating store of industrial offcuts for those who know their way around a sewing machine.

Best buys: Great food without pesticides or chemicals sold by salt-of-the-earth people. You could also visit a fortune teller and sample Uruguayan meat delicacies, why not!

When: 8am-3pm, Sunday – the 428 bus stops right outside.

Carriageworks Farmers Market

Why here: The bustling Carriageworks Farmers Market invades the open, attractive grounds of the Carriageworks theatre. The whole area pulses to an inner-city vibe. Over 70 farmers from NSW and the ACT set up shop here to show off their vibrant, fresh pickings.

Best buys: Artisan farmers produce such as cheeses, olive oils and salts.

When: 8am-1pm, Saturday.

Chinatown Night Market

Why here: Pop over to Asia, without leaving Sydney! The plumes of charcoal smoke coming from the roasting octopus skewers transports you to a night market in Southeast Asia. The huge variety of quality food on offer at Chinatown's Markets has a reputation for rivalling the markets of Bangkok and Hanoi.

Best buys: Tap into what's all-the-rage in Asia right now: new phone gadgets, toys and original wares from students and designers. But really, the food has to be eaten to be believed – make sure you arrive hungry.

When: 4-11pm, Friday.

Kirribilli Markets

Why here: The Harbour Bridge looming above you in a posh area where the Australian Prime Minister lives – come get fancy. Kirribilli Markets is one of Sydney's oldest and most popular markets with more than 220 stalls. If you've had a clear out, bring along your unwanted clothes to recycle here as the market is decked out with bins promoting responsible fashion.

Best buys: Seek out some vintage swanky label clothing or head to the Burton Street Tunnel section for top notch antiques with a Price tag to match.

When: 8.30am-3pm every fourth Saturday and second Sunday of the month (be sure to double check their dates when planning a visit).

Paddington Markets

Why here: Looking for an edgy, statement piece? Local artisans, jewellery, clothes and chocolate designers test their products here to a fashion-forward crowd. Paddington

Markets hasn't missed a Saturday since it started in 1973. Wear your Saturday best and bring your credit card.

Best buys: Up-and-coming unique clothing labels. Some big Australian brands started in these markets, such as Dinosaur Designs and Sass & Bide.

When: 10am-4pm, Saturday.

Rottnest Island: beyond the quokka selfies

Rottnest Island or Wadjemup (its Aboriginal name) has long been a playground for Perth's outdoorsy population. A short ferry ride across the Indian Ocean, Rottnest remains popular with locals and travellers alike. However there's more to Rotto (as it is colloquially referred to) than sandy beaches, cute quokkas and a laidback-holiday vibe. The island has a fascinating – and often grim – history to discover.

Bike to the beach and back

Aside from service vehicles, Rottnest Island is car-free. Roads are paved and the terrain not severely hilly, so the bicycle is king here. You'll see people on bikes, which are available for hire on the island, everywhere from The Settlement – the main town area in Thomson Bay where you'll arrive by ferry – to the island's most westward point.

While cycling Rottnest you may well spot the island's famous marsupial: the quokka. Technically nocturnal, near The Settlement these small furry creatures have learned to come out by day to eat food scraps left by tourists. Do resist the urge to feed them as human food is not great for their health. So many travellers pose for a selfie with one it has its own hashtag #quokkaselfie.

Though Rottnest is always popular, it isn't hard to find a quiet piece of its coastline to enjoy in relative peace. The jagged outline of the island contains a large number of bays and beaches, from long stretches of sand and aquamarine water, to tiny beaches fringed by rocks.

Of the best places to have a dip in the ocean, The Basin is close to The Settlement, and Ricey Beach is in the west. One of the nicest small beaches is at Little Parakeet Bay, close to the island's second township at Geordie Bay.

Water sports and walks

Surfing, bodyboarding and stand-up paddling are big on the island, with waves commonly two to three times higher here than at mainland locations. Strickland Bay is an acclaimed surfing break, along with Salmon Bay and Stark Bay.

Fishing is another popular aquatic activity, as Rotto's waters contain a variety of species. If you haven't brought your own fishing gear, you can hire or purchase it in The Settlement.

Underwater, you can see fish, coral and shipwrecks by joining a diving tour; though most of these operate from the mainland. An on-island alternative is the Rottnest Island

Snorkelling Cruise, which includes an hour of snorkelling in a selected bay.

If you'd rather explore on dry land, head out along the Wadjemup Bidi, a series of walking trails which take in natural highlights.

A challenging history

Before Rottnest was a holiday hotspot, it had a grim history as a colonial-era prison. From 1838 to 1904 it was used as a place of imprisonment for 3,700 Aboriginal men and boys.

These prisoners built much of the island's infrastructure, including the lighthouses. They were housed in the building known as the Quod. Until recently the Quod was used as accommodation, but there are plans to repurpose it, along with the nearby Aboriginal Burial Ground, as an official memorial to those who lived – and died – here. Visit the Rottnest Museum to learn more about this period.

Nearby is the Salt Store, a remnant from a period when salt was produced from Rottnest Island's salt lakes and transported to Fremantle. Rebuilt in 1997 to be used as a gallery and convention space, this store house was originally constructed by Aboriginal prisoners in 1868.

Rottnest also saw a flurry of activity during wartime. In World War I the island was used to house internees and prisoners of war, and in World War II massive guns were installed at the Oliver Hill Battery as protection should Perth come under attack.

Guides now give tours of these emplacements and the tunnels beneath. Get there via the Oliver Hill Train which follows the route of a former military railway, and enjoy the great views as it climbs.

To learn more about the island's brutal past, it's worth taking one of the free historic walking tours in The Settlement run by volunteer guides headquartered at the Salt Store. The 'Reefs, Wrecks and Daring Sailors' tour discusses the many shipwrecks of the place, and the local pilots who helped prevent them.

Still got time to kill?

If you're a golfer, you can try your luck (or skill) on the nine-hole course at the Rottnest Island Country Club. From November to April the Just 4 Fun Aqua Park, an inflated water park, floats on Thomson Bay. For a unique perspective of Rottnest Island you can also drop onto it from a great height with Skydive Geronimo.

Making it happen

Most people visit Rottnest as a day trip, but it can be rewarding to stay over and enjoy the serenity after the daytime crowds have departed. There are comfortable hotel rooms at both Karma Rottnest and the Hotel Rottnest; and there's a hostel within the old army barracks at Kingston.

To visit the island, catch a ferry operated by either Rottnest Express or Rottnest Fast Ferries.

The best free things to do in Adelaide

Found yourself in Adelaide with limited funds? Not to worry – there's plenty to see and do here that won't cost you a cent. In fact, the city's gratis offerings make a terrific introduction to local life and the surrounding scenery. Not to mention the fantastic climate – which the locals love to call 'Mediterranean' – well, that comes for free too.

From beautiful views and beach days, to guided walking tours and incredible art collections, the city has an abundance to offer in exchange for just your time and energy!

Free-wheeling ain't stealing

First thing's first, the best way to get the lay of the land is to hop on the bus. Adelaide has two free 'city loop' bus services, in effect providing a scenic tour of the city centre and surroundings for diddly-squat! The buses weave through the city in opposite directions and are as frequent as every 30 minutes. Get on board!

Another option for getting around town is the 'Adelaide Free Bikes' system run by Bicycle SA. Just bring a form of photo ID as your deposit in exchange for a rental bike – complete with helmet, lock and maps – and pedal around this big, smooth city. There are several pick-up hubs around town, the only catch being you must return the bike to the same location you borrowed it from. But hey, it's free!

Freedom on foot

For a more tailored tour experience, check out the Adelaide City Council's free downloadable Adelaide City Explorer self-guided walking tours. There are 19 themed trails available, zeroing-in on subjects like historic pubs, flora and fauna, art-deco architecture and public art.

For a loftier perspective of the Adelaide landscape – a vast urban plain hugged by the croissant-shaped Adelaide Hills – take a drive (or catch the bus) up to Mt Lofty Summit. The highest point in the hills that guard the city, this is a top spot to pick out Adelaide's landmarks and gaze wistfully towards the horizon at Gulf St Vincent.

A fabulous walking trail kicks off from the lookout, tracking 3.9km downhill to the aptly named Waterfall Gully. It's a steep but very well maintained bush track. There are a series of waterfalls along the route, but the biggest and best is First Falls at the bottom of the trail, which is extremely photogenic post rain shower.

Art and historical offerings

North Terrace, the broad avenue running across the northern edge of Adelaide's CBD, plays host to two of the city's estimable cultural bastions: the South Australian Museum and the Art Gallery of South Australia. Special and touring exhibitions incur admission fees, but unless you stop for coffee or lunch at one of the cafés (highly recommended), your visit will be free. Spending a few hours in each is the perfect way to beat the heat of the city streets.

South Australian Museum highlights include the mesmerising Australian Aboriginal Cultures galleries, which give focus to South Australian indigenous artefacts and heritage. Don't miss the incredible archival film footage showcased throughout the exhibitions. There's also the eye-popping Pacific Cultures Gallery, with its dazzling collection of masks, weapons, and traditional costumes from tribal groups across the region. Kids gravitate towards the impressive World Mammals display, with all and sundry hairy beasts safely imprisoned behind glass.

Right next door, the Art Gallery of South Australia has recently been transformed from a somewhat staid, old operator into something far more edgy. It's a long way from matching Hobart's MONA in the shock-and-awe stakes, but the vibe here these days is progressive and hip. The Australian Collection lures art buffs, with plenty of famous names – like Smart, McCubbin, Nolan, Whiteley and Tucker – to ogle in hushed parquetry-floored spaces.

Urban green space

An anomaly of Australian urban development, Adelaide was a planned city, laid out in a sensible, organised fashion in the 1830s by master planner, Colonel William Light. Part of Light's grand scheme was a band of green belts encircling the centre – think New York's Central Park, only in reverse. The park lands have survived the decades, offering space to enjoy the summer heat and more playgrounds, sports ovals and picnic spots than you could possibly investigate in one visit.

One park land gem is the free Adelaide Botanic Gardens – check out the giant waterlily pavilion and the seed-filled Museum of Economic Botany. Roam a little further and you'll find the spooky-but-fascinating West Terrace Cemetery, the final resting place for more than a few nefarious types. Or, just pull up a sunny patch of grass by the River Torrens near the Adelaide Festival Centre. Try to score a spot alongside the statue of Colonel William Light himself on Montefiore Hill, enjoy a picnic and count the ducks/joggers.

Life's a beach

For a fun, laidback budget experience, ride the tram to Glenelg – home to Adelaide's most popular beach, aka 'the Bay' – and splash around in the sea. In fact, Adelaide has a superb string of golden-sand beaches fronting onto Gulf St Vincent that manage to fly under the radar because, unlike those in

Sydney, Byron Bay and the Gold Coast, there's no surf. Appealingly though, the west-facing coast snares the afternoon sun, setting the scene for refreshing evening drinks and fish and chips on the sand. Glenelg also has a lengthy pier – perfect for an evening promenade before or after the aforementioned drink.

Before the sun sets, check out the free displays at the Bay Discovery Centre, including some amazing bits and pieces dredged up from the sea bed when the new pier replaced the old one (seemingly a handy spot to dispose of suspicious pistols).

The unexpected art of outback New South Wales

For many travellers to Oz, the state of New South Wales (NSW) has big-ticket appeal. Top billing goes to Sydney and the state's supercharged coastline, but its far-west outback corner often goes overlooked.

Out here, there is otherworldly beauty in the rough and rugged terrain, inspiring an eccentricity and creativity in a population whose artistic output belies its small size. In this off-the-beaten-track destination, art is found in the most unlikely places: on pub walls and rock faces, down opal mines and atop desert hills, in paddocks miles from anywhere.

Broken Hill

Broken Hill (population 18,500) is the 'capital' of the NSW outback region, lying 1150km from Sydney. It's a desert frontier town built on mining, so it's tough as nails and full of archetypal 'blokiness' – but it has surprisingly soft edges too, including creativity and community spirit in abundance. There's nation-defining history here, too – in January 2015, Broken Hill became the first and only entire Australian town to be included on the National Heritage List. As a hot and dusty mining town, you better believe there are plenty of classic old pubs where you can wet your whistle.

However, fun fact: Broken Hill has more art galleries than pubs. A great place to begin an art-hop is the Broken Hill Regional Art Gallery, housed in a beautifully restored emporium dating from 1885. It's the oldest regional gallery in the state and holds 1800 works in its permanent collection, by Australian masters like John Olsen, Sidney Nolan and Arthur Streeton, as well as strong indigenous representation.

Broken Hill was home to the 'Brushmen of the Bush', a celebrated group of five artists who took paintings of outback Australia to the world. The works (and art collection) of former miner Kevin Charles 'Pro' Hart (1928-2006) are on display at the engrossing Pro Hart Gallery – check out his Rolls Royce collection, including one Pro painted with scenes from Australian history.

Not far away is the gallery of another Brushman; Jack Absalom's Gallery is a purpose-built space attached to octogenarian Jack's home. His canvases beautifully capture the light and color of outback landscapes, and you can admire (as well as purchase) opals mined by the artist.

One unmissable town landmark is the Palace Hotel – you may have seen it take a starring role in the movie The Adventures of Priscilla, Queen of the Desert. This three-storey pub was erected on the main street in 1889; inside, wonderfully kitsch landscape murals cover almost every inch of the public areas. They're described as 'Italian Renaissance meets Outback' and were painted in the 1970s by indigenous artist, Gordon Waye. The pub owner's only stipulation to Waye was that each scene contain a water feature so the hotel would feel like an oasis in the outback. It still feels that way – there's a restaurant, retro accommodation, Friday night two-up games and the classic outback essential: cold beer.

As the sun sets, pack a picnic and watch the sky turn crimson from the 2400 hectare Living Desert State Park 12km outside town. Here, perched on a view-enriched summit, you'll find the 'sculpture symposium': a range of sculptures created by 12 international artists in 1993. The artists (some local, others from as far afield as Mexico, Syria and Georgia) carved the huge sandstone blocks on site.

Silverton

Creativity and quirk flow from every dusty corner of Silverton, 25km west of Broken Hill and reached through kangaroo- and emu-dotted desertscapes. It's home to about 50 people, a handful of wandering donkeys, a colourful (and character-filled) pub as well as a museum dedicated to the movie Mad Max 2 (yes, you've read that right). Visiting is like stepping into one of Australian artist Russell Drysdale's stark and evocative paintings. Or indeed a classic 'cowboys and Indians' film set: Silverston has been the location for more movies than almost anywhere else in Australia (the pub has the inside scoop).

Alongside these endearing eccentricities, Silverston also has an inspiring, thriving art community. Outback-inspired works (jewellery, photography, painting, ceramics, found art – some serious, some fun) are exhibited in a handful of postcard-worthy art galleries.

Mutawintji National Park

This vast, spectacular national park lies 130km northeast of Broken Hill. Indigenous Australians have lived in the area for thousands of years, and there is a rich collection of ancient Aboriginal rock art, including important engravings and hand stencils, plus scattered remains of their day-to-day life. Many of these are protected within the Mutawintji Historic Site, which is only accessible with a guide. There are some excellent tours to choose between, operating from Broken Hill.

Lightning Ridge

Like other outback mining communities, the ramshackle town of Lightning Ridge throws up quality characters and gems alike. It's one of the world's few sources of valuable black opals, and several of the Ridge's underground mines and opal showrooms are open to the public.

Our favorite is the remarkable Chambers of the Black Hand, where artist and miner Ron Canlin has turned a 40ft-deep mining claim into a cavernous gallery of carvings and paintings: superheroes, celebrities, pharaohs, buddhas, animals, you name it. The ornate abyss is equal parts tacky and inspired.

The Ridge is a hugely entertaining place to spend a few days – pick up a handout from the visitor centre and follow the four self-drive 'car door' tours, which explore different areas of interest around town. Each tour is marked by coloured car doors (green, blue, yellow and red), demonstrating the community's ingenuity and wit. Call in to the John Murray Art Gallery for more clever and irreverent takes on outback life.

Utes in the paddock

Not quite in the NSW outback but heading there, Utes in the Paddock is a one-of-a-kind art installation, and a fun tribute to Australian pastoral life. As its name suggests, the 'art' lies in a paddock about 70km from the town of Parkes, heading west on the Condobolin road. Here, 20 iconic vehicles (only Holdens!) have been given a creative makeover. Admire UteZilla (an oversized metallic kangaroo), the Emute (a vehicle painted in emu heads), the TribUte (covered in indigenous art), and one ute designed to resemble a toilet cubicle with Dame Edna on the loo.

Capital cuisine: a gourmet guide to Canberra

Despite national monuments and surrounding vineyards, Canberra is eternally overlooked in favour of Australia's other major cities. Best known for diplomats, parliamentary sessions and war memorials, the city never stood a chance against icon-studded Sydney or culture-rich Melbourne. But Canberra's critics are stepping down, as its food scene flourishes into something truly worth travelling for...

Canberra's encircling meadows and well-groomed vines place local produce on the city's doorstep. Sky-high standards for coffee, cocktails and fine dining have nurtured a restaurant scene with an exclusive feel. From farm-fresh produce to fusion cuisine, here are four ways to sample Canberra's up-and-coming food scene.

Get buzzed on Canberran coffee

It barely needs stating that Australian cities know their coffee, but Canberra is aiming for top billing. Sample the coffee scene in Braddon, an inner-north suburb adored by local gourmands and foodstagrammers. Start with a velvety-smooth flat white at Barrio, where milks are given as much thought as the coffee beans (only locally sourced dairy milk, or nut milks creamed in-house, will do).

Just beating Barrio in the perfectionism stakes is Ona Coffee. This speciality coffee brewer's baristas inform you which of the beans suit milky coffees (and decline to add milk to those deemed unsuitable – it'd be a waste of premium beans, after all). Of Ona's outlets, the Cupping Room has won countless plaudits, but we're also fans of Manuka, where silky brews are served alongside modern-rustic brunches like chicken and quinoa tabbouleh, or field mushrooms on toast with a tangy slick of goat cheese curd.

Carbs are essential to offset the caffeine shakes, and this being Canberra, that means artisan bread. Head to Silo Bakery, purveyor of the best sourdough in Canberra, or award-winning Three Mills, whose bread is studded with walnut or raisin and orange.

Nourish body and soul at farm-to-table restaurants

With such a porous boundary between city and country, locally sourced dining is all the rage in Canberra – and it sprouts at all levels, from budget cafes to high-class restaurants.

At the cheerfully cheap end of the scale is Canberra institution the Food Co-op Shop – part organic veggie seller, part wholefoods cafe. There are decades of history behind this co-op, which has long battled to serve affordable, healthy food to students. These days its raw cakes and vegan lunches are a community experience. Pick up pesticide-free sweetcorn or zucchini (unpackaged, of course) while you're here.

More upmarket is Mocan & Green Grout, in the restaurant-packed precinct of NewActon. Their well-balanced brunches are created from local produce, as is their beautiful steak tartare – with ingredients sourced from down the road, even nervous diners might dare to try this raw meat and egg dish.

Swish a glass in local wineries

Around 140 vineyards snooze in Canberra's wine region, many of them draped alongside the roads north of the city. Rieslings have particularly venerable beginnings, first planted in nearby New South Wales vineyards in 1838.

Helm Wines, 40km north of the city, has scooped up accolades for their citrus-scented riesling. The family-run vineyard is managed by descendants of generations of vine-dressers from Rhineland (appropriately enough, the German birthplace of the riesling grape). Helm's award-winning wines are best swigged in their 19th-century tasting room, a former schoolhouse.

Helm is one in a crown of wineries in Murrumbateman, a sleepy former gold mining and wheat-growing village turned boutique winery hub. Another worthy stop is Murrumbateman Winery, established during the village's 1970s wine boom. If a cheese platter sounds too cliché an accompaniment to their dry, appley riesling, Murrumbateman Winery also serves scones.

Local shiraz is almost as acclaimed in Canberra's wine region; make for Yarrh Wines, nestled in bushland 7km northeast of Murrumbateman. Their plummy, small-batch shiraz wines are somehow tastier in the glow of their eco-conscious practices (such as a naturally cooled sunken cellar and passive solar design).

The trouble with out-of-town wineries is that you need a car to reach them. Fortunately back in the city, tucked-away Canberra Wine House curates the best of the region – like Lerida Estate's floral pinot gris and peppery Four Winds shiraz – on its menu. So after one too many 'what's grüner veltliner, anyway?' moments, you can stagger into a taxi bound for your hotel.

Pair cocktails with fusion cuisine

Befitting Canberra's community of diplomats and expats, the restaurant scene is a grab-bag of international cuisines. The downside? Some restaurants justify high Prices by OTT presentation and stiff service. However, plenty of restaurants strike the right tone and, for a city accused of being a goody-two-shoes, some of them feel pretty naughty, too...

Faux-industrial Jones & Co has a classic Canberra vibe, with marble-topped bars as polished as the service. Kingfish ceviche and oysters are whisked from the raw bar, and sharing plates of soft-shell crab and blue-cheese gnocchi keep grazers going for hours. Menu tip: 'bigger share plates' translates to 'the size of your head'.

But Canberra's dining scene is most stimulating where the line blurs between restaurant and boozer. Another trendy Braddon venue is Korean-fusion food and cocktail joint Lazy Su. Vegan glass-noodle salads and moreish pork bao are freshened by cocktails like matcha-infused pisco sour and aperol with yuzu (an aromatic citrus fruit). Just south is psychedelic diner Akiba, whose cocktails – wasabi martini, and banana, sake and rose water – embrace the menu's Japanese flavours. On the opposite side of the globe (but only a short walk west) is Spanish-themed Temporada, a highly acclaimed tapas and wine haunt in a sleek, warehousey interior. From Australia to Spain via Asia: the perfect gourmet globetrot to finish a capital weekend in Canberra.

Beyond the rock: the best experiences around Uluru

Making the pilgrimage to Australia's most iconic rock is an essential travel experience. While there are now a variety of ways to experience Uluru (Ayers Rock) in a culturally sensitive and responsible manner, there are also plenty of other off-the-beaten-path attractions in the Northern Territory desert to really get the most of your trip.

Get ready to rock and roll through the Red Centre experiencing stunning climbs and hikes, a wealth of fascinating culture and history as well as a handful of quirky festivals and events.

Exploring the other rocks

Uluru might be the key draw of visiting Australia's Red Centre, but it's not the only big rock out there. Roughly 30km from the most renowned rubble in Uluru-Kata Tjuta National Park, the 36 striking red domes of Kata Tjuta (The Olgas) are well worth a journey. Kata Tjuta means 'many heads', and is of great tjukurpa (relating to Aboriginal law, religion and custom) significance. It is for this reason that only two walks remain open to tourists: the short and beautiful Walpa Gorge walk (2.6km return, 45 minutes), and the more challenging but rewarding Valley of the Winds loop (7.4km, between two and four hours). Tourists are urged to stay on the tracks, and climbing on the boulders is not permitted.

Like Uluru, Kata Tjuta looks particularly beautiful at sunset, and the dune viewing platform is a fantastic place to be during sunrise, when the morning sun crests directly behind majestic Uluru in the distance. The domes can be visited independently with your park entry ticket ($25), or on one of many tours that can be booked through Ayers Rock Resort.

And then there's 'Fool-uru'. Known as Uluru's forgotten rock, Atila (Mt Conner) was formed during the same period of uplift that created its likeness approximately 550 million years ago. The majestic mesa sits on Curtin Springs cattle station, 80km north of Uluru. Tourists were once allowed to drive freely through the area, but following one rescue too many, the station owners enlisted the help of local operator SEIT Outback Australia to run tours from Uluru.

On a half-day 4WD tour of the property, you'll visit the spectacular salt flats of Lake Swanson, featuring free-roaming cattle and feral camels (half a million camels are thought to run wild in the Aussie outback!) on your way to get a close-up of Atila. If you decide to grab dinner at Curtin Springs on the way back to Uluru, you might be lucky enough to meet iconic local character Peter Severin, who set up the station with his wife Dawn in 1956.

Learning about Aboriginal culture

It would be remiss to leave Uluru without taking time to learn more about its deep spiritual and cultural significance to the Anangu, Uluru's traditional custodians. The excellent Cultural Centre (and attached Walkatjara Art Centre) near the foot of Uluru, and the base walk itself (the daily Mala Walk is often led by indigenous guides) both offer fascinating insights, but the opportunities don't stop there.

Ayers Rock Resort offers half a dozen cultural experiences ranging from free garden walks and dot painting workshops, to the on-site Mani-Mani Cultural Theatre which screens the story of Aboriginal ancestral beings, Walawuru, Kakalyalya and Kaanka.

Next to the Desert Gardens Hotel, the Wintjiri Arts & Museum provides a glimpse into the region's history, geology, flora and fauna, showcasing Anangu-made art and products. The Mulgara Gallery in the foyer of Sails in the Desert hotel exhibits fascinating indigenous art and craft. Local artists also sell pieces at the daily art market held in the resort's modest 'town square'.

Intrigued? It's currently possible to visit private Aboriginal lands on two 4WD drive tours offcrcd by Uluru Family Tours that can be booked through SEIT Outback Australia. The Patji Tour allows you to explore Anangu Country with a member of the Uluru family. You will visit sacred sites, try your hand at traditional food gathering, and learn about the family's struggle for land rights. On the Cave Hill Tour you will visit one of the most significant rock art sites in Central Australia accompanied by an Anangu guide, who will teach you about its tjukurpa.

Hiking Kings Canyon

Located 300km from Uluru, it is entirely possible to hike the legendary Kings Canyon in Watarrka National Park on a day trip from Ayers Rock area. If you're driving and hope to do the famous 6km Rim Walk (between three and four hours), aim to arrive before 9.00am on days forecast to hit 36°C, when rangers close the gates for safety reasons.

If you don't have your own set of wheels, you can book a return guided hiking tour with AAT Kings, who also offer onward passage to Alice Springs (320km north) at the end of the day. The tour stops at quirky Kings Creek Station for breakfast (where you can stock up on bottles of water if you haven't already brought the required three litres), and the plush Kings Canyon Resort for lunch following the hike.

The Rim Walk begins with a steep, challenging climb (ominously nicknamed 'Heart Attack Hill'), but once you reach the peak it's a relatively easy amble through spectacular landscapes including the beehive-like domes of the so-called 'Lost

City', followed by the lush oasis at the heart of the canyon known as the Garden of Eden. Those looking for a less strenuous walk may prefer the 2km Creek Bed Walk (one hour), which highlights impressive views of the canyon periphery.

If you are driving, there's also the Kathleen Springs Walk, a 2.6km (1.5 hour) return walk to a waterhole, situated just down the road from Kings Canyon. Serious hikers can head for the Giles Track, a 22km route, typically undertaken as an overnight hike. Like Uluru and Kata Tjuta, part of the gorge is a sacred Aboriginal site and visitors are discouraged from straying from the walking tracks.

Attending festivals and special events

Cooler autumn climates spell festival season in Uluru, kicking off with the Tjungu Festival in April, which celebrates the best of Australian indigenous culture with lively markets, musical performances, delicious culinary experiences and sports events. At the end of the May there's Uluru's Camel

Cup, with plenty of entertainment both on and off the racetrack. Ayers Rock Resort also hosts a changing roster of special events, from astronomer-in-residence programs and yoga retreats, to British artist Bruce Munro's exquisite Field of Light exhibition, which runs until the end of March 2018.

Driving the Gibb River Road: an Australian Outback adventure

Taking its complete circuit-of-the-country, Highway 1, in its Great Northern Highway guise, skirts along the southern boundary of the Kimberley region. Between Derby and Kununurra the road runs through Fitzroy Crossing and Halls Creek, but if you want to really get to grips with what is arguably the country's most authentically 'Australian' region then you have to abandon that comfortably smooth thoroughfare and tackle the Gibb River Road.

It runs through the heart of the Kimberley and is 125 miles (200km) shorter, but way slower. It can be a car-breaker. Tackle the Gibb River Road in wet conditions and you can be stuck there waiting for a river to subside. Tackle it in the dry after a long spell without a grader coming through and the notorious corrugations can shake the fillings out of your teeth and rattle your car down to its component parts.

Assorted early explorers touched on the convoluted, inlet-cut, island-dotted coastline of the Kimberley, and today a convoy of adventure travel boats shuttle along this spectacular shoreline. Inland, the Kimberley is something of an open-air gallery of amazing Aboriginal rock art, whether it's the comparatively recent Wandjina paintings or the much older and still puzzling Bradshaw works. The English name comes from Joseph Bradshaw, a late-1800s pastoralist turned rock-art hunter who first categorised and labelled the paintings.

Today they're called Gwion Gwion paintings, but it's uncertain how old they are or even who did them – today's Aboriginals sometimes comment that they're 'not by our mob'. Bradshaw paintings are usually in 'galleries', often rock faces protected by overhangs, while the Wandjina works may be in everyday living areas. The later Wandjina figures are more varied in their subject matter, their design and their colours, but lack the subdued, calm elegance of the Bradshaw figures.

The secret of a successful foray along the Gibb River Road is to take your time, not to hurry. Drive too fast and those corrugations, loose stones, unexpected potholes and sharp edges can shred a tyre in seconds. This is a route where a second spare can be a very good idea. It's not just travelling slowly that can stretch the time, lots of the Gibb River Road attractions are excursions off the main route. You can add days to the trip if you plan to turn off south to the Mornington Camp, or if you head north up the road towards Kalumburu and then decide to divert to the Mitchell Falls.

Close to the Kununurra end of the road is El Questro, with its magnificent gorges and places to stay that range all the way from budget campsites to the luxurious Homestead, which is dramatically perched on a cliff edge above the Chamberlain Gorge. El Questro started out as a Kimberley cattle station and although today it's the best example of combining four-legged and two-legged business, for a number of the Gibb River Road cattle stations tourists are today just as important as 'beasts'.

Travelling east, Derby on the coast is the place to stock up, fuel up, admire the boabs – the Kimberley's signature tree – and enjoy the last stretch of bitumen before the rough stuff starts. Ninety miles (144km) from Derby is the turn-off to the dazzling Windjana Gorge and then Tunnel Creek, you can follow this track all the way to the Great Northern Highway, intersecting it not far west of Fitzroy Crossing. Don't plan to visit these sites in the wet season, but in the dry they're a vital diversion.

There's a campsite at Windjana Gorge and more places to stay at Mt Hart Wilderness Lodge and Charnley River, but many Gibb River Road travellers turn south to visit the Australian Wildlife Conservancy's Mornington Camp near the Fitzroy River. The camp makes a great base to explore over a thousand square miles (3000 square km) of stunning gorges, creeks and waterholes. In between paddling canoes along Annie Creek, visitors can dine under the stars or front the outback bar for a refreshing cold beer. As ever, Australia's outback night sky can offer an extravagant backdrop, while birdwatchers can add their ticks to the checklist of more than 200 bird species which have been spotted in the sanctuary.

The halfway point comes up soon after the Mt Barnett Roadhouse, followed by the turn-off north to the Drysdale River Station and, almost up at the coast, the Kalumburu Aboriginal community. Another turn from that road takes you down an often very rough track past the Mitchell Plateau airstrip to the Mitchell Falls. They are worth the effort. Tumbling down from one pool to another, these are the most spectacular waterfalls in Australia. There are also swimming opportunities in the pools, as there are at other gorges and waterholes throughout the Kimberley. Of course, you have to keep an eye out for crocodiles at certain locations, but usually it's the reasonably friendly freshwater variety. Only on the way down towards the coast, well away from the Gibb River Road, do you encounter the distinctly less friendly saltwater crocodiles.

In the dry season there's usually a helicopter or two waiting to offer flightseeing trips over the Mitchell Falls. Helicopters also run from the Mitchell Plateau airstrip to the

Kimberley Coastal Camp, one of the most remote Kimberley outposts which, if you can afford the entry cost, attracts near fanatical enthusiasts. Finally, there's Ellenbrae and assorted rivers – including the Durack River and the Pentecost River – to ford just before you reach El Questro. Soon after this final taste of the Kimberleys there's bitumen road to signal that it's not far to go to civilisation once again at the town of Kununurra.

Step out of the car

It's a Gibb River Road surprise that you often find excuses to abandon your car for alternative transport. This could be your feet on the many interesting walking tracks; exploring the gorges by canoe, kayak or boat at Mornington Camp or El Questro (where horses are also on offer); or, if your credit card will stretch far enough, helicopters. Banking down those Kimberley gorges around El Questro in a chopper is simply mind-blowing.

Directions

Start – Derby, Western Australia; end – Kununurra, Western Australia; distance – 440 miles (704km)

Getting there: Broome (138 miles, 220km from Derby) and Darwin (517 miles, 827km from Kununurra) are the major gateways to the region, though there are flights to Kununurra.

When to drive: Not when the wet season kicks in around November, unless you've got the experience to ford deep rivers and the patience to wait if they really are too deep. The road dries out by April.

Where to stay: Bring your camping gear. However, some places offer more permanent accommodation, including real luxury at El Questro.

What to take: A 4WD, though when the road is good a rugged car can tackle it with enough ground clearance.

Experiences in Australia

Sydney

Sydney, spectacularly draped around its glorious harbour and beaches, has a visual wow factor like few other cities. Scratch the surface and it only gets better.

On the Wild Side

National parks ring the city and penetrate right into its heart. Large chunks of harbour are still bush-fringed, while parks cut their way through skyscrapers and suburbs. Consequently, native critters turn up in the most surprising places. Clouds of flying foxes pass overhead at twilight and spend the night rustling around in suburban fig trees; oversized spiders stake out corners of lounge-room walls; possums rattle over roofs of terrace houses; and sulphur-crested cockatoos screech from the railings of urban balconies. At times Sydney's concrete jungle seems more like an actual one – and doesn't that just make it all the more exciting?

After Dark

After a lazy Saturday at the beach, urbane Sydneysiders have a disco nap, hit the showers and head out again. There's always a new restaurant to try, undercover bar to hunt down, hip band to check out, sports team to shout at, show to see or crazy party to attend. The city's pretensions to glamour are well balanced by a casualness that means a cool T-shirt and a tidy pair of jeans will get you in most places. But if you want to dress up and show off, there's plenty of opportunity for that among the sparkling harbour lights.

Making a Splash

Defined just as much by its rugged Pacific coastline as its exquisite harbour, Sydney relies on its coastal setting to replenish its reserves of charm; venture too far away from the water and the charm suddenly evaporates. Jump on a ferry and Sydney's your oyster – the harbour prises the city's two halves far enough apart to reveal an abundance of pearls. On the coast, Australia ends abruptly in sheer walls of sandstone punctuated by arcs of golden sand. In summer they're covered with bronzed bodies making the most of a climate that encourages outdoor socialising, exercising, flirting and fun.

Show Pony

Brash is the word that inevitably gets bandied around when it comes to describing the Harbour City, and let's face it, compared to its Australian sister cities, Sydney is loud, uncompromising and in your face. Fireworks displays are more dazzling here, heels are higher, bodies more buffed, contact sports more brutal, starlets shinier, drag queens glitzier and Prices higher. Australia's best musos, foodies, actors, stockbrokers, models, writers and architects flock to the city to make their mark, and the effect is dazzling: a hyperenergetic, ambitious, optimistic and unprincipled marketplace of the soul, where anything goes and everything usually does.

Experiences in Sydney

Sydney Opera House

Top choice notable building in Circular Quay & The Rocks

Price - tours adult/child $37/20

Hours - tours 9am-5pm

Contact - http://www.sydneyoperahouse.com; 02-9250 7111

Location - Bennelong Point, Sydney, Australia

Designed by Danish architect Jørn Utzon, this World Heritage–listed building is Australia's most famous landmark. Visually referencing a yacht's sails, it's a soaring, commanding presence. The complex comprises five performance spaces for dance, concerts, opera and theatre. The best way to experience the building is to attend a performance, but you can also take a one-hour guided tour. Ongoing renovation work, scheduled to be completed in 2021, may disrupt visits.

There's also a two-hour 'access all areas' backstage tour ($169), which departs at 7am and includes breakfast in the Green Room.

Sydney Harbour National Park

Top choice national park in Sydney Harbourside

Contact - http://www.nationalparks.nsw.gov.au

Sydney Harbour National Park protects large swathes of bushland around the harbour shoreline, plus several harbour islands. In among the greenery you'll find walking tracks, scenic lookouts, Aboriginal carvings, beaches and a handful of historic sites. The park incorporates South Head and Nielsen Park on the south side of the harbour, but most of the park is on the North Shore – including Bradleys Head, Middle Head, Dobroyd Head and North Head.

Bondi Beach

Top choice beach in Bondi, Coogee & the Eastern Beaches

Location - Campbell Pde, Sydney, Australia

Definitively Sydney, Bondi is one of the world's great beaches. It's the closest ocean beach to the city centre (8km away), has consistently good (though crowded) waves, and is great for a rough-and-tumble swim (the average water temperature is a considerate 21°C). If the sea's angry, try the child-friendly saltwater sea baths at either end of the beach.

Two surf clubs – Bondi and North Bondi – patrol the beach between sets of red-and-yellow flags, positioned to avoid the worst rips and holes. Thousands of unfortunates have to be rescued from the surf each year (enough to make a TV show about it), so don't become a statistic – swim between the flags.

Surfers carve up sandbar breaks at either end of the beach; it's a good place for learners, too. Changing rooms and lockers (small/large $4/6) can be found at Bondi Pavilion.

Gay guys tend to hang out near the North Bondi Surf Club, which is also where there's an outdoor workout area. At the beach's northern end there's a grassy spot with coin-operated barbecues, but don't bring booze to your picnic – it's banned on the beach.

Sydney Harbour Bridge

Top choice bridge in Circular Quay & The Rocks

Location - Sydney, Australia

Sydneysiders love their giant 'coathanger', which opened in 1932. The best way to experience this majestic structure is on foot. Stairs climb up the bridge from both shores, leading to a footpath on the eastern side (the western side is a bike path). Climb the southeastern pylon to the Pylon Lookout or ascend the arc on the popular but expensive BridgeClimb.

The harbour bridge is a spookily big object – moving around town you'll catch sight of it in the corner of your eye, sometimes in the most surprising of places. Its enormous dimensions make it the biggest (if not the longest) steel arch bridge in the world.

The two halves of chief engineer JJC Bradfield's mighty arch were built outwards from each shore. In 1930, after seven years of merciless toil by 1400 workers, the two arches were only centimetres apart when 100km/h winds set them swaying. The coathanger hung tough and the arch was finally bolted together. Extensive load-testing preceded the bridge's opening two years later.

Royal Botanic Garden

Gardens in Circular Quay & The Rocks

Hours - 7am-dusk

Contact - http://www.rbgsyd.nsw.gov.au;
02-9231 8111

Location - Mrs Macquarie's Rd, Sydney,
Australia

Southeast of the Opera House, this garden
was established in 1816 and features plant
life from around the world. Within the
gardens are hothouses with palms and ferns,

as well as the Calyx, a striking exhibition space featuring a curving glasshouse gallery with a wall of greenery and temporary plant-themed exhibitions. Grab a park map at any main entrance.

The gardens include the site of the colony's first paltry vegetable patch, but their history goes back much further than that; long before the convicts arrived, this was an initiation ground for the Gadigal (Cadigal) people. Free 1½-hour guided walks depart at 10.30am daily, plus 1pm on weekdays (no 1pm tour from December to February). Book ahead for an Aboriginal Heritage Tour.

A hop-on, hop-off tourist train runs a route around the main points of interest in the garden.

Art Gallery of NSW

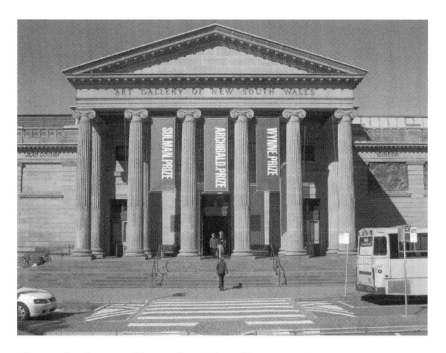

Top choice gallery in City Centre & Haymarket

Hours - 10am-5pm Thu-Tue, to 10pm Wed

Contact - http://www.artgallery.nsw.gov.au; 1800 679 278

Location - Art Gallery Rd, Sydney, Australia

With its neoclassical Greek frontage and modern rear, this much-loved institution plays a prominent and gregarious role in Sydney society. Blockbuster international touring exhibitions arrive regularly and there's an outstanding permanent collection of Australian art, including a substantial Indigenous section. The gallery also plays host to lectures, concerts, screenings, celebrity talks and children's activities. A range of free guided tours is offered on different themes and in various languages; enquire at the desk or check the website.

While the permanent collection has a strong collection of 19th-century European and Australian art, the highlights are the contemporary Indigenous gallery in the basement, and the collection of 20th-century Australian art, with some standout canvases by the big names of the local painting scene. Look out for Albert Tucker's scary Apocalyptic Horse, Russell Drysdale's brilliant gold-town street Sofala and half a room full of Sidney Nolans, usually including one or more of his extraordinary

Ned Kelly paintings. There's a good representation of female artists too, including Grace Cossington Smith and several Margaret Olleys on rotation. Arthur Boyd works include his terracotta sculpture of Judas Kissing Christ, while Brett Whiteley is represented by the intoxicatingly blue harbour of The Balcony 2.

The unfailingly controversial Archibald Prize for Australian portraiture exhibits here annually, as do the Wynne Prize (landscape or figure sculpture), the Sulman Prize (subject or mural painting), and the Artexpress exhibition of the year's best school-student art.

The cafe and restaurant are fine places to hang out, with outdoor seating and views over Woolloomooloo Bay. Wednesday nights are fun too, with talks, live music and other events.

Construction of a second building was approved in 2017 and is due to be completed in 2021. Occupying space to the north of the existing building, it's a major project, to be known as Sydney Modern, that will be centred around a new Indigenous gallery and a dedicated space for major touring exhibitions. The construction work shouldn't affect gallery visits.

Quay

Modern australian in Circular Quay & The Rocks

Price - 4/8 courses $180/245

Hours - 6-9.30pm Mon-Thu, noon-1.30pm & 6-9.30pm Fri-Sun

Contact - http://www.quay.com.au; 02-9251 5600

Location - L3, Overseas Passenger Terminal, Sydney, Australia

What many consider to be Sydney's best restaurant matches a peerless Bridge view with brilliant food. Chef Peter Gilmore never rests on his laurels, consistently delivering exquisitely crafted, adventurous cuisine. The menu was set to be shaken up in 2018; you can rely on amazing creations. Book online well in advance, but it's worth phoning in case of cancellations.

Taronga Zoo Sydney

Zoo in Sydney Harbourside

Price - adult/child $46/26

Hours - 9.30am-5pm Sep-Apr, to 4.30pm May-Aug

Contact - http://www.taronga.org.au; 02-9969 2777

Location - Bradleys Head Rd, Sydney, Australia

A 12-minute ferry ride from Circular Quay, this bushy harbour hillside is full of kangaroos, koalas and similarly hirsute

Australians, plus numerous imported guests. The zoo's critters have million-dollar harbour views, but seem blissfully unaware of the privilege. Encouragingly, Taronga sets benchmarks in animal care and welfare. Highlights include the nocturnal platypus habitat, the Great Southern Oceans section and the Asian elephant display. Feedings and encounters happen throughout the day, while in summer, twilight concerts jazz things up (see www.twilightattaronga.org.au).

Tours include Nura Diya; Roar & Snore is an overnight family experience. There's also Wild Ropes, high ropes courses offering special views (it's cheaper to buy this with zoo entry than separately).

Catching the ferry is part of the fun. From the wharf, the Sky Safari cable car or a bus will whisk you to the main entrance, from which you can traverse the zoo downhill back to the ferry. Disabled access is good, even when arriving by ferry.

If you are driving and staying a while, note that the zoo car park ($18 per day) is much cheaper than the metered parking on the streets around (weekdays/weekends $4.20/7 per hour). Getting here by bus is the cheapest option; the 247 heads here from Wynyard.

West Head

Top choice national park in Sydney

Price - per car $12

Hours - 6am-6pm Apr-Sep, 6am-8.30pm Oct-Mar

Contact - http://www.nationalparks.nsw.gov.au; 02-9472 8949

Location - West Head Rd, Sydney, Australia

This central section of Ku-ring-gai Chase National Park is a spectacular wilderness, with awe-inspiring vistas over Pittwater and Broken Bay, hidden beach communities, Aboriginal engravings and great walking tracks down to perfect little coves. It's accessed off Mona Vale Rd in Terrey Hills or via boat from Palm Beach. West Head itself, 14km from the main road, offers a sensational lookout point and a precipitous trail down to a WWII emplacement. Other trailheads are signposted along the road.

The West Head lookout sees you gazing eastwards over the Palm Beach peninsula or north to Lion Island and across Broken Bay to Umina and Pearl Beach.

About 3.5km short of West Head is the Basin Track, which offers an easy stroll to a good set of Indigenous engravings. Approximately 2.5km further along the track is the Basin, a shallow round inlet where there is a beach (day visitors adult/child $3/2) and camping area. Access is via this track or by boat from Palm Beach. A branch off the Basin Track heads down to the remote, carless beachside suburbs of Mackerel Beach and Currawong (Little Mackerel) Beach, also accessible by ferry from Palm Beach.

About 1km short of West Head, the Resolute picnic area has faint Indigenous ochre handprints nearby at Red Hands Cave. Also from here, the Resolute Track, heads past an Aboriginal engraving site on a 3km loop that takes in pretty Resolute Beach and another site. You can push on a little (some wading required) to Mackerel Beach, allowing you to return via the Basin Track.

Normally elusive, lyrebirds are conspicuous at West Head during their mating season, from May to July.

Accessed via the same exit off Mona Vale Rd are the pretty Pittwater locales of Church Point, Akuna Bay and Cottage Point, all bristling with bobbing leisure boats. All have eating options. The scenic road winding along the water is curiously named after the liberator of Argentina, General José de San Martín. Apparently it was a reciprocal gesture after a Buenos Aires street was named Australia.

There are no buses into the park. The only public transport to reach it are the ferries from Palm Beach. Cycling is a good option around the park's roads, but it's a long ride to here from the nearest station. Bus 270 goes from downtown Sydney to Terrey Hills; you could head on from there by taxi, Uber or perhaps bike-share.

Ku-ring-gai Chase National Park

Top choice national park in Sydney

Price - per car per day $12, landing fee by boat adult/child $3/2

Hours - sunrise-sunset

Contact - http://www.nationalparks.nsw.gov.au; 02-9472 8949

Location - Sydney, Australia

This spectacular 14,928-hectare park, 20 to 30km from the city centre, forms Sydney's northern boundary. It's a classic mix of sandstone, bushland and water vistas, taking in over 100km of coastline along the southern edge of Broken Bay, where it heads into the Hawkesbury River. There are two unconnected principal sections, Bobbin Head and the West Head area. The Barrenjoey headland at Palm Beach is also part of the park.

Ku-ring-gai, declared in 1894, takes its name from its original inhabitants, the Guringai people, who were all but wiped out just after colonisation through violence at the hands of settlers and the devastating introduction of smallpox. It's well worth reading Kate Grenville's The Secret River for an engrossing but harrowing telling of this story.

Remnants of Aboriginal life are visible today thanks to the preservation of more than 800 sites, including rock paintings, middens and cave art.

Elevated park sections offer glorious water views over Cowan Creek, Broken Bay and Pittwater.

For information about the park, stop at the Bobbin Head Information Centre, operated by the NSW National Parks & Wildlife Service. Also here are a marina, picnic areas, a cafe and a boardwalk leading through mangroves.

Access to the park is by car – McCarrs Creek Rd (Terrey Hills) for West Head; Bobbin Head Rd (North Turramurra) or Ku-ring-gai Chase Rd (Mount Colah) for Bobbin Head – the Palm Beach Ferry or water taxi.

Chinatown

Top choice area in City Centre & Haymarket

Contact - http://www.sydney-chinatown.info

Location - Sydney, Australia

Dixon St is the heart of Chinatown: a narrow, shady pedestrian mall with a string of restaurants and insistent spruikers. The ornate dragon gates (paifang) at either end have fake bamboo tiles, golden Chinese calligraphy and ornamental lions to keep evil spirits at bay. Chinatown in general (not necessarily just between the dragon gates) is a fabulous eating district, which effectively extends for several blocks north and south of here, and segues into Koreatown and Thaitown to the east.

This is actually Sydney's third Chinatown: the first was in the Rocks in the late 19th century before it moved to the Darling Harbour end of Market St. Dixon St's Chinatown dates from the 1920s. Look for the fake-bamboo awnings guarded by dragons, dogs and lions, and kooky upturned-wok lighting fixtures.

On Hay St, the Golden Water Mouth sculpture represents a symbolic fusion of China and Australia. A little further down Hay St, Paddy's Markets fills the lower level of a hefty brick building. It started out in the mid-19th century with mainly European traders, but these days the tightly packed market stalls are more evocative of present-day Vietnam. Beyond Paddy's Markets, there's some great cheap eating to be done in the area around Thomas and Quay Streets and Ultimo Road.

Melbourne

Stylish, arty Melbourne is both dynamic and cosmopolitan, and it's proud of its place as Australia's sporting and cultural capital.

Within the Grid

It's long been commented that Melbourne's inner city is the most European of any in Australia; the leafy eastern section of Collins St was dubbed the 'Paris end' in the 1950s. There's a bit of New York in the mix as well, thanks to the city's well-ordered grid and scattering of art-deco high-rises. But Melbourne is uniquely Melbourne and a lot of that's down to the more than 230 laneways that penetrate into the heart of the city blocks. It's here that the inner city's true nature resides, crammed into narrow lanes concealing world-beating restaurants, bars and street art.

Neighbourhoods

Melbourne is best experienced as a local would, with its character largely reliant upon its diverse collection of inner-city neighbourhoods. Despite a long-standing north–south divide (flashy South Yarra versus hipster Fitzroy), there's a coolness about its bars, cafes, restaurants, festivals and people that transcends the borders. Ethnic communities have gravitated together in some areas, and Melburnians know to head to Victoria St in Richmond for Vietnamese food, Lygon St in Carlton for old-school Italian, Balaclava for Jewish bakeries, Brunswick for Middle Eastern,

Footscray for African and Chinatown for all manner of Asian cuisines.

Sport

It's not the high-rises and bridges that strike you when you first visit Melbourne but the vast sporting edifices that fringe the city centre. Melburnians are passionate about AFL football ('footy'), cricket and horse racing, while grand-slam tennis and Formula One car racing draw visitors in droves. Sport is a crucial part of the social fabric, taking on something of a religious aspect here. In fact, sporting events have nearly as many public holidays allotted to them as religion – everyone gets the day off for the Melbourne Cup horse race and the Friday before the AFL Grand Final!

Deep Reserves of Cool

Melbourne was 'hipster' before the word was ever attached to bearded 20-something Bon Iver fans. It's long had an artsy, liberal, bohemian and progressive strand to its subculture, and coffee and food have been obsessions here for decades. Word spreads about interesting new eateries and, before you know it, queues are forming outside. The international trend for faux-speakeasy bars is redundant in Melbourne as the city has had edgy places hidden down laneways and on warehouse rooftops for many years. Melbourne doesn't have to try hard – it just is.

Experiences in Melbourne

Royal Botanic Gardens

Top choice gardens in South Yarra, Prahran & Windsor

Hours - 7.30am-sunset

Contact - http://www.rbg.vic.gov.au

Location - Birdwood Ave, Melbourne, Australia

Melbourne's Royal Botanical Gardens are simply glorious. From the air, the 94-acre spread evokes a giant green lung in the middle of the city. Drawing over 1.5 million visitors annually, the gardens are considered one of the finest examples of Victorian-era landscaping in the world. You'll find a global selection of plantings and endemic Australian flora. Mini ecosystems, such as a cacti and succulents area, a herb garden and an indigenous rainforest, are set amid vast lawns.

In summer the gardens play host to Moonlight Cinema and theatre performances. Other features include the 19th-century Melbourne Observatory for tours of the night sky, and the excellent, nature-based Ian Potter Foundation Children's Garden, a whimsical, child-scaled place that invites kids and their parents to explore, discover and imagine.

The visitor centre is the departure point for tours, some of which are free and all of which should be booked by calling ahead (see the website for details). Close by, the National Herbarium, established in 1853, contains over a million dried botanical specimens used for plant-identification purposes.

For visitors who can't get enough, the Royal Botanical Gardens has recently developed the Australian Garden in the outlying suburb of Cranbourne.

Hosier Lane

Top choice public art in City Centre

Location - Melbourne, Australia

Melbourne's most celebrated laneway for street art, Hosier Lane's cobbled length draws camera-wielding crowds snapping edgy graffiti, stencils and art installations. Subject matter runs to the mostly political and countercultural, spiced with irreverent humour; pieces change almost daily (not even a Banksy is safe here). Be sure to see Rutledge Lane (which horseshoes around Hosier), too.

NGV International

Top choice gallery in Southbank & Docklands

Hours - 10am-5pm

Contact - http://www.ngv.vic.gov.au; 03-8662 1555

Location - 180 St Kilda Rd, Melbourne, Australia

Housed in a vast, brutally beautiful, bunkerlike building, the international branch of the National Gallery of Victoria has an expansive collection that runs the gamut from the ancient to the bleeding edge. Regular blockbuster exhibitions (Prices vary) draw the crowds, and there are free 45-minute highlights tours at 11am and 1pm daily, and hour-long tours at midday and 2pm.

Key works include a Rembrandt self-portrait, Tiepolo's The Banquet of Cleopatra and Turner's otherworldly Falls of

Schaffhausen. It's also home to Picasso's Weeping Woman, which was the victim of an art heist in 1986. The 1st floor is given over to Asian art, with exquisite pieces from China, Japan, India and Southeast Asia. The gallery also has an excellent decorative arts and furniture collection, which is showcased alongside contemporaneous paintings rather than being quarantined in its own section.

Designed by architect Sir Roy Grounds, the NGV building was controversial when it was completed in 1967 but has come to be respected as a modernist masterpiece. Make sure you wander through the foyer to the Great Hall, with its extraordinary stained-glass ceiling, and continue out onto the sculpture lawn.

The NGV's Australian art collection is on display at the Ian Potter Centre at nearby Federation Sq.

Melbourne Cricket Ground

Top choice stadium in Richmond & East Melbourne

Price - tour adult/child/family $23/12/55, incl museum $32/16/70

Hours - tours 10am-3pm

Contact - http://www.mcg.org.au; 03-9657 8888

Location - Brunton Ave, Melbourne, Australia

With a capacity of 100,000 people, the 'G' is one of the world's great sporting venues, hosting cricket in summer and AFL (Australian Football League; Aussie rules) footy in winter. For many Australians it's considered hallowed ground. Make it to a game if you can (highly recommended), but otherwise you can still make your pilgrimage on nonmatch-day tours that take you through the stands, media and coaches' areas, change rooms and members' lounges. The MCG houses the state-of-the-art National Sports Museum.

In 1858 the first game of Aussie Rules football was played where the MCG and its car parks now stand, and in 1877 it was the venue for the first test-cricket match between Australia and England. The MCG was the central stadium for the 1956 Melbourne Olympic Games, two Cricket World Cups and the 2006 Commonwealth Games. It was also used as an army barracks during WWII. Despite this venerable history, the oldest parts of the existing structure are the light towers, dating from the 1980s.

The stadium is ringed by gigantic sporting sculptures facing the tidy lawns of Yarra

Park. Also look out for the scarred tree, whose bark was removed in pre-colonial times by the local Wurundjeri people for artisanal purposes.

Shrine of Remembrance

Monument in South Yarra, Prahran & Windsor

Hours - 10am-5pm

Contact - http://www.shrine.org.au; 03-9661 8100

Location - Birdwood Ave, Melbourne, Australia

One of Melbourne's icons, the Shrine of Remembrance is a commanding memorial to Victorians killed in WWI. Built between 1928 and 1934, much of it with Depression-relief, or 'susso' (sustenance), labour, its stoic, classical design is partly based on the Mausoleum of Halicarnassus, one of the seven ancient wonders of the world. The shrine's upper balcony affords epic panoramic views of the Melbourne skyline and all the way up tram-studded Swanston St.

This unobstructed view isn't coincidental; planning regulations continue to restrict any building that would encroach on the view of the shrine from Swanston St as far back as Lonsdale St.

The shrine itself draws thousands to its annual Anzac Day (25 April) dawn service, while the Remembrance Day service at 11am on 11 November commemorates the signing of the 1918 Armistice marking the formal end to WWI. At this precise moment a shaft of light shines through an opening in the ceiling, passing over the Stone of Remembrance and illuminating the word 'love'; on all other days this effect is demonstrated using artificial lighting on the hour.

With its cenotaph and eternal flame (lit by Queen Elizabeth II in 1954), the forecourt was built as a memorial to those who died in WWII, and several other specific memorials surround the shrine. Below the shrine, a stunningly conceived architectural space houses the Galleries of Remembrance, a museum dedicated to telling the story of Australians at war via its 800-plus historical artefacts and artworks.

The complex is under 24-hour police guard; during opening hours the police are quaintly required to wear uniforms resembling those worn by WWI light-horsemen. Download the free Shrine of Remembrance app for a self-guided tour, or consider joining the free guided tours daily at 11am and 2pm, often conducted by returned soldiers.

Melbourne Zoo

Zoo in North Melbourne & Parkville

Price - adult/child $36/18, child weekends & holidays free

Hours - 8am-5pm

Contact - http://www.zoo.org.au; 1300 966 784

Location - Elliott Ave, Melbourne, Australia

Established in 1861, this compact zoo is the oldest in Australia and the third oldest in the world. It remains one of the city's most popular attractions and it continues to innovate, recently becoming the world's first carbon-neutral zoo. Set in prettily landscaped gardens, the zoo's enclosures aim to simulate the animals' natural habitats and give them the option to hide if they want to (the gorillas and the tigers are particularly good at playing hard to get).

There's a large collection of native animals in natural bush settings, a platypus aquarium, fur seals, plenty of reptiles, and an entire faux–South East Asian jungle village built around the elephant enclosures.

In some cases walkways pass through the enclosures: you can stroll through some of the aviaries and enter a tropical hothouse full of colourful butterflies. See if you can pass through Lemur Island without an internal soundtrack of 'I like to move it, move it' turning over in your mind. Sadly, the lion enclosure remains out of bounds.

In summer, the zoo hosts twilight concerts, while from September to May Roar 'n' Snore (adult/child $190/150) allows you to camp at the zoo and join the keepers on their morning feeding rounds.

Melbourne Museum

Top choice museum in Carlton & Brunswick

Price - adult $15, child & student free, exhibitions extra

Hours - 10am-5pm

Contact - http://www.museumvictoria.com.au; 13 11 02

Location - 11 Nicholson St, Melbourne, Australia

This museum provides a grand sweep of Victoria's natural and cultural histories, incorporating dinosaur fossils, giant-squid specimens, a taxidermy hall, a 3D volcano and an open-air forest atrium of Victorian flora. Become immersed in the legend of champion racehorse and national hero Phar Lap. The excellent Bunjilaka, on the ground floor, presents Indigenous Australian stories and history told through objects and Aboriginal voices with state-of-the-art technology. There's also an IMAX cinema.

Royal Exhibition Building

Top choice historic building in Carlton & Brunswick

Price - tours adult/child $10/7

Contact - http://www.museumvictoria.com.au/reb; 13 11 02

Location - 9 Nicholson St, Melbourne, Australia

Built for the 1880 International Exhibition, and winning Unesco World Heritage status in 2004, this beautiful Victorian edifice symbolises the glory days of the Industrial Revolution, the British Empire and 19th-century Melbourne's economic supremacy. It was the first building to fly the Australian flag, and Australia's first parliament was held here in 1901; it now hosts everything from trade fairs to car shows. Tours of the building leave from Melbourne Museum (opposite) at 2pm.

Justin Art House Museum

Top choice gallery in South Yarra, Prahran & Windsor

Price - adult/child $25/free

Hours - by appointment

Contact - http://www.jahm.com.au; 0411 158 967

Location - cnr Williams Rd & Lumley Ct, Melbourne, Australia

The geometric, zinc-clad home of Melbourne art collectors Charles and Leah Justin doubles as the Justin Art House Museum. Book ahead for a private tour of the couple's dynamic collection of contemporary art, consisting of more than 250 pieces amassed over four decades. There's a strong emphasis on video and digital art, with the works rotated regularly. Guided tours take around two hours. The house was designed by the couple's daughter, Elisa.

Brisbane

No longer satisfied in the shadow of Sydney and Melbourne, Brisbane is subverting stereotypes and surprising the critics. Welcome to Australia's new subtropical 'It kid'.

Alfresco Living, Year-round

Brisbane has a climate its more famous southern rivals would kill for (despite what they may tell you). When Sydney and Melbourne shiver through the winter months, Brisbane continues basking in the sun. After all, this is the capital city of the Sunshine State, a meteorological Promised Land where winters are mild and short enough for a daytime alfresco toast. It's a fact not lost on Brisbanites, who indulge in outdoor thrills all year round, from inner-city rock-climbing and kayaking, to riverside cycling and sunning on the nation's only man-made city beach.

Culinary Enlightenment

The Brisbane food scene is booming. Innovation and ingenuity are the key words these days, driving everything from Gauge's cult-status black garlic bread to Nodo's Valrhona chocolate and beetroot dougnuts. Menus across the city are flaunting the seasonal and the regional, transforming top-notch produce into beautiful, confident dishes spanning all budgets and countless cuisines. Imbibing in Brisbane is no less impressive, with a sharp, competent booty of specialty coffee microroasteries, microbreweries and cocktail bars pouring faultless single-origin brews, seasonal beers and out-of-the-box cocktails crafted with everything from lemon myrtle to local Brisbane honey.

Cultural Awakenings

Forget the 'cultural backwater' tag. Brisbane 2.0 is a kicking hub of creativity, with an expanding arsenal of enlightening, thought-provoking drawcards. It's here that you'll find the Australia's largest public gallery of modern art (GOMA), its most important festival of new Australian music (Bigsound Festival), not to mention one of its most innovative and enlightened annual film festivals (the Brisbane Asia Pacific Film Festival). Whether you're up for catching a cult-status band in a state-of-the-art hangar, a subversive cabaret in a one-time power station, or an opera in a subterranean reservoir, this town has you covered.

Experiences in Brisbane

Gallery of Modern Art

Top choice gallery in South Bank

Hours - 10am-5pm

Contact - http://www.qagoma.qld.gov.au

Location - Stanley Pl, Brisbane, Australia

All angular glass, concrete and black metal, must-see GOMA focuses on Australian art from the 1970s to today. Continually changing, and often confronting, exhibits range from painting, sculpture and photography to video, installation and film. There's also an arty bookshop, children's activity rooms, a cafe, a Modern Australian restaurant, as well as free guided gallery tours at 11am, 1pm and 2pm.

South Bank Parklands

Park in South Bank

Hours - dawn-dusk

Contact - http://www.visitbrisbane.com.au

Location - Grey St, Brisbane, Australia

Should you sunbake on a sandy beach, chill in a rainforest, or eye-up a Nepalese peace pagoda? You can do all three in this 17.5-hectare park overlooking the city centre. Its canopied walkways lead to performance spaces, lush lawns, eateries and bars, public art and regular free events ranging from yoga sessions to film screenings. The star attractions are Streets Beach, an artificial, lagoon-style swimming beach (packed on weekends); and the near-60m-high Wheel of Brisbane, delivering 360-degree views on its 10-minute rides.

Also in the parklands is Stanley St Plaza, a renovated section of historic Stanley St lined with mainstream cafes, restaurants, a handful of shops and a bustling pub. On Friday night, Saturday and Sunday, the plaza hosts the tourist-heavy Collective Markets South Bank, peddling everything from artisan leather wallets and breezy summer frocks, to prints, skincare and contemporary handmade jewellery.

Close by, Courier-Mail Piazza is an outdoor performance space offering free, year-round events.

City Hall

Top choice landmark in Central Brisbane

Hours - 8am-5pm Mon-Fri, 9am-5pm Sat & Sun, clock tower tours 10.15am-4.45pm, City Hall tours 10.30am, 11.30am, 1.30pm & 2.30pm

Contact - http://www.brisbane.qld.gov.au; 07-3339 0845

Location - King George Sq, Brisbane, Australia

Fronted by a row of sequoia-sized Corinthian columns, this sandstone behemoth was built between 1920 and 1930. The foyer's marble was sourced from the same Tuscan quarry as that used by Michelangelo to sculpt his David. The Rolling Stones played their first-ever Australian gig in the building's auditorium in 1965, a magnificent space complete with a 4300-pipe organ, mahogany and blue-gum floors and free concerts every Tuesday at noon. Free tours of the 85m-high clock tower run every 15 minutes; grab tickets from the excellent on-site Museum of Brisbane.

For a more comprehensive exploration of Australia's largest city hall, opt for the 45-minute guided tour of the building (which includes access to the clock tower). Although tickets for this tour should be booked in advance by phone, they are often available on the day from the Museum of Brisbane counter, so always consider checking.

Story Bridge Adventure Climb

Adventure sports in Kangaroo Point & Woolloongabba

Price - climb from $100

Contact - http://www.sbac.net.au; 1300 254 627

Location - 170 Main St, Brisbane, Australia

Scaling Brisbane's most famous bridge is nothing short of thrilling, with unbeatable views of the city – morning, twilight or night. The two-hour climb scales the southern half of the structure, taking you 80m above the twisting, muddy Brisbane River below. Dawn climbs are run on the last Saturday of the month. Minimum age 10 years.

Mt Coot-tha Lookout

Viewpoint in Brisbane

Hours - 24hr

Contact - http://www.brisbanelookout.com;
07-3369 9922

Location - 1012 Sir Samuel Griffith Dr,
Brisbane, Australia

You'll be surveying the Brisbane skyline and
greater metro area from this lofty lookout
within Mt Coot-tha Reserve. Choose a clear
day and you'll even spot the Moreton Bay
islands.

Eat Street Markets

Street food in Brisbane

Price - admission adult/child $2.50/free, meals from $10

Hours - 4-10pm Fri & Sat

Contact - http://www.eatstreetmarkets.com; 07-3358 2500

Location - 99 MacArthur Ave, Brisbane, Australia

What was once a container wharf is now Brisbane's hugely popular take on the night food market. Its maze of shipping-containers-turned-kitchens peddle anything from freshly shucked oysters to smoky American barbecue and Turkish gözleme. Add craft brews, festive lights and live music and you have one of Brisbane's coolest nights out. To get here, catch the CityCat ferry to Bretts Wharf.

Eat Street Markets also operates during the day on Sunday in the cooler months; see the website for dates and times.

Perth

Laid-back, liveable Perth has wonderful weather, beautiful beaches and an easygoing character. About as close to Bali as to some of Australia's eastern state capitals, Perth combines big-city attractions and relaxed, informal surrounds, providing an appealing lifestyle for locals and lots to do for visitors. It's a sophisticated, cosmopolitan city, with myriad bars, restaurants and cultural activities all vying for attention. When you want to chill out, it's easy to do so. Perth's pristine parkland, nearby bush, and river and ocean beaches – along with a good public-transport system – allow its inhabitants to spread out and enjoy what's on offer.

Why Go?

Basking under a near-permanent canopy of blue sky, Perth is a modern-day boom town, stoking Australia's economy from its glitzy central business district. Anchored by the broad Swan River flowing past skyscrapers and out to the Indian Ocean, the city boasts recent developments like Elizabeth Quay and Perth Stadium, which have added a more cosmopolitan sheen to this traditionally laid-back town.But Perth's heart is still down at the beach, tossing in clear surf and relaxing on the sand. The city's beaches trace the western edge of Australia for around 40km, and on any given day you can often have one all to yourself. Perth has sprawled to enfold Fremantle within in its suburbs, but the raffish port town with a great food and arts scene maintains its own distinct personality – immensely proud of its nautical ties, working-class roots and bohemian reputation.

Experiences in Perth

Kings Park & Botanic Garden

Top choice park in Perth

Hours - guided walks 10am, noon & 2pm

Contact - http://www.bgpa.wa.gov.au; 08-9480 3600

Location - Perth, Australia

Rising above the Swan River on the city's western flank, the 400-hectare, bush-filled expanse of Kings Park is Perth's pride and joy. At the park's heart is the 17-hectare Botanic Garden, containing over 2000 plant species indigenous to WA. In spring there's an impressive display of the state's famed wildflowers. A year-round highlight is the Lotterywest Federation Walkway, a 620m path including a 222m-long glass-and-steel bridge that passes through the canopy of a stand of eucalypts.

The main road leading into the park, Fraser Ave, is lined with towering lemon-scented gums that are dramatically lit at night. At its culmination are the State War Memorial, a cafe, a gift shop, Fraser's restaurant and the Kings Park Visitor Centre. Free guided walks leave from here.

It's a good spot for a picnic or to let the kids off the leash in one of the playgrounds. Its numerous tracks are popular with walkers and joggers all year round, with an ascent of the steep stairs from the river rewarded with wonderful views from the top.

The Noongar people knew this area as Kaarta Gar-up and used it for thousands of years for hunting, food gathering, ceremonies, teaching and toolmaking. A freshwater spring at the base of the escarpment, now known as Kennedy Fountain but before that as Goonininup, was a home of the Wargal, mystical snakelike creatures that created the Swan River and other waterways.

To get here take bus 935 from St Georges Tce to near the visitor centre. You can also walk up (steep) Mount St from the city or climb Jacob's Ladder from Mounts Bay Rd, near the Adelphi Hotel.

Art Gallery of Western Australia

Top choice gallery in Perth

Hours - 10am-5pm Wed-Mon

Contact - http://www.artgallery.wa.gov.au;
08-9492 6622

Location - Perth, Australia

Founded in 1895, this excellent gallery
houses the state's pre-eminent art collection.
It contains important post-WWII works by

Australian luminaries such as Arthur Boyd, Albert Tucker, Grace Cossington Smith, Russell Drysdale, Arthur Streeton and Sidney Nolan. The Indigenous-art galleries are also very well regarded: work ranges from canvases to bark paintings and sculpture, and artists include Rover Thomas, Angilya Mitchell, Christopher Pease and Phyllis Thomas. Check the website for info on free tours running most days at 11am and 1pm.

The annual WA Indigenous Art Awards entries are displayed here from August to December.

Cottesloe Beach

Beach in Perth

Location - Marine Pde, Perth, Australia

The safest swimming beach, Cottesloe has cafes, pubs, pine trees and fantastic sunsets. From Cottesloe train station (on the Fremantle line) it's 1km to the beach. Bus 102 ($4.60) from Elizabeth Quay Busport goes straight to the beach.

Aquarium of Western Australia

Aquarium in Perth

Price - adult/child $30/18

Hours - 10am-5pm

Contact - http://www.aqwa.com.au; 08-9447 7500

Location - Hillarys Boat Harbour, 91 Southside Dr, Perth, Australia

Dividing WA's vast coastline into five distinct zones (Far North, Coral Coast, Shipwreck Coast, Perth and Great Southern), AQWA features a 98m underwater tunnel showcasing stingrays, turtles, fish and sharks. (The daring can snorkel or dive with the sharks with the aquarium's in-house dive master.) By public transport, take the Joondalup train to Warwick station and then transfer to bus 423. By car, take the Mitchell Fwy north and exit at Hepburn Ave.

Diving costs $159 with your own gear (to hire snorkel/dive gear add $20/40). Behind-the-scenes tours (per person $95) run at 11am Thursday and Saturday. Bookings are essential.

Bell Tower

Landmark in Perth

Price - adult/child $18/9

Hours - 10am-4pm, ringing noon-1pm Sat-Mon & Thu

Contact - http://www.thebelltower.com.au; 08-6210 0444

Location - Barrack Sq, Perth, Australia

This pointy glass spire fronted by copper sails contains the royal bells of London's St Martin-in-the-Fields, the oldest of which dates to 1550. The bells were given to WA by the British government in 1988, and are the only set known to have left England. Clamber to the top for 360-degree views of Perth by the river.

The tower sits on land that was reclaimed in the 1920s and 1930s and now forms a green strip between the river and the city. Long, thin Langley Park is still occasionally used as an airstrip for light-aircraft demonstrations. Nearby Stirling Gardens and Supreme Court Gardens have lawns and formal gardens that fill up with city workers at lunchtime.

Elizabeth Quay

Area in Perth

Contact - http://www.elizabethquay.com.au

Location - Perth, Australia

A vital part of the city's urban development is the Elizabeth Quay area taking shape at the bottom of Barrack St. Luxury hotels and apartments are under construction, joining recently opened waterfront restaurants. With a busport, train station and ferry terminal, the area is also developing as a transport hub. Current highlights include the spectacular Elizabeth Quay pedestrian bridge.

Across summer the area hosts food trucks and various pop-up events and is very popular with local families.

Perth Zoo

Zoo in Perth

Price - adult/child $29/14

Hours - 9am-5pm

Contact - http://www.perthzoo.wa.gov.au; 08-9474 0444

Location - 20 Labouchere Rd, Perth, Australia

Part of the fun of a day at the zoo is getting there – taking the ferry across the Swan River from Elizabeth Quay Jetty to Mends Street Jetty (every half-hour) and walking up the hill. Zones include Reptile Encounter, African Savannah (rhinos, cheetahs, zebras, giraffes and lions), Asian Rainforest (elephants, tigers, sun bears, orangutans) and Australian Bushwalk (kangaroos, emus, koalas, dingos). Another transport option is bus 30 or 31 from Elizabeth Quay Busport.

Perth Institute of Contemporary Arts

Gallery in Perth

Hours - 10am-5pm Tue-Sun

Contact - http://www.pica.org.au; 08-9228 6300

Location - Perth, Australia

PICA (pee-kah) may look traditional – it's housed in an elegant 1896 red-brick former school – but inside it's one of Australia's principal platforms for contemporary art, including installations, performance, sculpture and video. PICA actively promotes new and experimental art, and it exhibits graduate works annually. From 10am Tuesday to Sunday, the PICA Bar is a top spot for a coffee or cocktail, and has occasional live music.

Adelaide

Sophisticated, cultured, neat-casual – the self-image Adelaide projects, a nod to the days of free colonisation without the 'penal colony' taint. Adelaidians may remind you of their convict-free status, but the stuffy, affluent origins of the 'City of Churches' did more to inhibit development than promote it. Bogged down in the old-school doldrums and painfully short on charisma, this was a pious, introspective place.

But these days things are different. Multicultural flavours infuse Adelaide's restaurants; there's a pumping arts and live-music scene; and the city's festival calendar has vanquished dull Saturday nights. There are still plenty of church spires here, but they're hopelessly outnumbered by pubs and a growing number of hip bars tucked away in lanes.

Just down the tram tracks is beachy Glenelg: Adelaide with its guard down and boardshorts up. Nearby Port Adelaide is slowly gentrifying but remains a raffish harbour 'hood with buckets of soul.

Experiences in Adelaide

Central Market

Top choice market in Adelaide

Hours - 7am-5.30pm Tue, 9am-5.30pm Wed & Thu, 7am-9pm Fri, 7am-3pm Sat

Contact - http://www.adelaidecentralmarket.com.au; 08-8203 7494

Location - Gouger St, Adelaide, Australia

A tourist sight, or a shopping op? Either way, satisfy your deepest culinary cravings at the 250-odd stalls in superb Adelaide

Central Market. A sliver of salami from the
Mettwurst Shop, a crumb of English Stilton
from the Smelly Cheese Shop, a tub of
blueberry yoghurt from the Yoghurt Shop –
you name it, it's here. Good luck making it
out without eating anything. Adelaide's
Chinatown is right next door. Adelaide's
Top Food & Wine Tours offers guided tours.

Exeter Hotel

Top choice pub in Adelaide

Hours - 11am-late

Contact - http://www.theexeter.com.au; 08-8223 2623

Location - 246 Rundle St, Adelaide, Australia

Adelaide's best pub, this legendary boozer attracts an eclectic brew of postwork, punk and uni drinkers, shaking the day off their backs. Pull up a bar stool or nab a table in the grungy beer garden and settle in for the evening. Original music nightly (indie, electronica, acoustic); no pokies. Book for curry nights in the upstairs restaurant (usually Wednesdays).

Adelaide Oval

Top choice landmark in Adelaide

Price - tours adult/child $22/12

Hours - tours 10am, 11am & 2pm daily, plus 1pm Sat & Sun

Contact - http://www.adelaideoval.com.au; 08-8205 4700

Location - King William Rd, Adelaide, Australia

Hailed as the world's prettiest cricket ground, the Adelaide Oval hosts interstate and international cricket matches in summer, plus national AFL football and state football matches in winter. A wholesale redevelopment has boosted seating capacity to 50,000 – when they're all yelling, it's a serious home-town advantage! Guided 90-minute tours run on nongame days, departing from the Riverbank Stand (south entrance), off War Memorial Dr: call for bookings or book online.

Also here is the Bradman Collection, where devotees of Don Bradman, cricket's greatest batsman, can pore over the minutiae of his legend, on loan from the State Library of South Australia. Check out the bronze statue of 'the Don' cracking a cover drive out the front of the stadium. Also here is Roofclimb Adelaide Oval, where you scale the giant roof scallops above the hallowed turf (amazing views!).

Art Gallery of South Australia

Top choice gallery in Adelaide

Hours - 10am-5pm

Contact - http://www.artgallery.sa.gov.aul;
08-8207 7000

Location - North Tce, Adelaide, Australia

Spend a few hushed hours in the vaulted,
parquetry-floored gallery that represents the
big names in Australian art. Permanent

exhibitions include Australian, Aboriginal and Torres Strait Islander, Asian, European and North American art (20 bronze Rodins!). Progressive visiting exhibitions occupy the basement. There are free guided tours (11am and 2pm daily) and lunchtime talks (12.30pm every day except Tuesday). There's a lovely cafe out the back too.

Governor Hindmarsh Hotel

Top choice live music in Adelaide

Hours - 11am-late

Contact - http://www.thegov.com.au; 08-8340 0744

Location - 59 Port Rd, Adelaide, Australia

Ground zero for live music in Adelaide, 'The Gov' hosts some legendary local and international acts. The odd Irish band fiddles around in the bar, while the main venue features rock, folk, jazz, blues, salsa, reggae and dance. A huge place with an inexplicably personal vibe. Good food too.

Orana

Modern australian restaurants in Adelaide

Price - tasting menus lunch/dinner $80/175, wine extra $75/150

Contact - http://www.restaurantorana.com; 08-8232 3444

Location - upstairs, 285 Rundle St, Adelaide, Australia

Racking up plenty of 'Adelaide's Best Restaurant' awards, Orana is a secretive beast, with minimal signage and access via a black staircase at the back of Blackwood restaurant on Rundle St. Upstairs a fab tasting menu awaits: at least seven courses for lunch, and 18 for dinner (18!). Add wine to the experience to fully immerse yourself in SA's best offerings.

Adelaide Botanic Gardens

Gardens in Adelaide

Hours - 7.15am-sunset Mon-Fri, from 9am Sat & Sun

Contact - http://www.botanicgardens.sa.gov.au; 08-8222 9311

Location - cnr North Tce & East Tce, Adelaide, Australia

Meander, jog or chew through your trashy airport novel in these lush city-fringe gardens. Highlights include a restored 1877 palm house, the water-lily pavilion (housing the gigantic Victoria amazonica), the First Creek wetlands, the engrossing Museum of Economic Botany and the fabulous steel-and-glass arc of the Bicentennial Conservatory (10am to 4pm), which re-creates a tropical rainforest. Free 1½-hour guided walks depart the Schomburgk Pavilion at 10.30am daily. The classy Botanic Gardens Restaurant is here too.

South Australian Museum

Museum in Adelaide

Hours - 10am-5pm

Contact - http://www.samuseum.sa.gov.au;
08-8207 7500

Location - North Tce, Adelaide, Australia

Dig into Australia's natural history with the
museum's special exhibits on whales and
Antarctic explorer Sir Douglas Mawson. An

Aboriginal Cultures Gallery displays artefacts of the Ngarrindjeri people of the Coorong and lower Murray. Elsewhere, the giant squid and the lion with the twitchy tail are definite highlights. Free tours depart 11am weekdays and 2pm and 3pm weekends. The cafe here is a handy spot for lunch/recaffeination.

Adelaide Park Lands

Gardens in Adelaide

Hours - 24hr

Contact - http://www.adelaideparklands.com.au; 08-8203 7203

Location - Adelaide, Australia

The city centre and ritzy North Adelaide are surrounded by a broad band of parkland. Colonel William Light, Adelaide's controversial planner, came up with the concept, which has been both a blessing and a curse for the city. Pros: heaps of green space, clean air and playgrounds for the kids. Cons: bone dry in summer, loitering perverts and a sense that the city is cut off from its suburbs.

Don't miss the playgrounds and Adelaide-Himeji Garden on South Tce, and the statue of Colonel William Light overlooking the Adelaide Oval and city office towers from Montefiore Hill.

Adelaide Zoo

Zoo in Adelaide

Price - adult/child/family $34.50/19/88.50

Hours - 9.30am-5pm

Contact -
http://www.zoossa.com.au/adelaide-zoo; 08-
8267 3255

Location - Frome Rd, Adelaide, Australia

Around 1800 exotic and native mammals, birds and reptiles roar, growl and screech at Adelaide's wonderful zoo, dating from 1883. There are free walking tours half-hourly (plus a slew of longer and overnight tours), feeding sessions and a children's zoo. Wang Wang and Fu Ni are Australia's only giant pandas and always draw a crowd (panda-monium!). Other highlights include the nocturnal and reptile houses. You can take a river cruise to the zoo on Popeye.

Newcastle

The port city of Newcastle may be one-10th the size of Sydney, but Australia's second-oldest city punches well above its weight. Superb surf beaches, historical architecture and a sun-drenched climate are only part of its charm. Fine dining, hip bars, quirky boutiques, a diverse arts scene and a laid-back attitude combine to make it well worth a couple of days of your time.

Newcastle had a rough trot at the end of the 20th century, with a major earthquake and the closure of its steel and shipbuilding industries. Its other important industry, shipping coal, has a decidedly sketchy future too, but Novocastrians always seem to get by with creative entrepreneurship and a positive attitude.

Experiences in Newcastle

Newcastle Art Gallery

Top choice gallery in Newcastle

Hours - 10am-5pm Tue-Sun

Contact - http://www.nag.org.au; 02-4974 5100

Location - 1 Laman St, Newcastle, Australia

Ignore the brutalist exterior, as inside this remarkable regional gallery are some wonderful works. There's no permanent exhibition; displays rotate the gallery's excellent collection, whose highlights include art by Newcastle-born William Dobell and John Olsen as well as Brett Whiteley and modernist Grace Cossington Smith.

Olsen's works, in particular, bring an explosive vibrancy to the gallery, with his generative organic swirls flamboyantly representing water-based Australian landscapes. Look out for his ceiling painting by the central stairwell and his brilliant King Sun and the Hunter, a tribute to the essence of his native city, painted at age 88 in 2016.

Newcastle Maritime Museum

Top choice museum in Newcastle

Price - adult/child $10/5

Hours - 10am-4pm Tue-Sun

Contact - http://www.maritimecentrenewcastle.org.au; 02-4929 2588

Location - Lee Wharf, 3 Honeysuckle Dr, Newcastle, Australia

Newcastle's nautical heritage is on show at this museum, appropriately located on the harbour. The intriguing exhibition provides an insight into the soul of the city, and there's a good dose of local history, covering shipwrecks (including the 2007 grounding of the Pasha Bulker, on which there's a film), lifeboats and the demise of the steelworks and shipbuilding industries. A quick intro by the staff is great for setting the scene.

Merewether Aquarium

Top choice public art in Newcastle

Location - Henderson Pde, Newcastle,
Australia

Not an aquarium in the traditional sense, this
pedestrian underpass has been charmingly
transformed into a pop-art underwater world
by local artist Trevor Dickinson. There are
numerous quirky details, including the artist

himself as a diver. Find it at the southern end of Merewether Beach, opposite the Surfhouse top entrance.

Newcastle Beach

Beach in Newcastle

Location - Newcastle, Australia

Surfers and swimmers adore this picturesque patrolled beach at the eastern end of the town centre. Nearby accommodation and eating options mean that you can base yourself here.

Hunter Wetlands Centre

Nature reserve in Newcastle

Price - adult/child $5/2

Hours - 9am-4pm

Contact - http://www.wetlands.org.au; 02-4951 6466, 1300 465 636

Location - 1 Wetlands Pl, Newcastle,
Australia

Transformed from a dump and abandoned
sporting fields into a magnificent
conservation sanctuary, this swampy centre
is home to over 200 species of bird,
including magpie geese, freckled ducks and
egrets, and a huge diversity of animal
residents. Extensive walking and bike trails
criss-cross the site, or you can hire a canoe
($10/3 per adult/child for two hours, last hire
1.30pm) and paddle along picturesque
Ironbank Creek.

Popular Segway tours ($65, Sundays, must
be pre-booked) are also a fun way to quietly
view the animals. The centre is off Sandgate
Rd. To get here, take the Pacific Hwy
towards Maitland and turn left at the
cemetery, or catch the train to Sandgate and
walk (10 minutes). There's a cafe on site
(open 10am to 2pm weekdays, 9.30am to
2.30pm weekends).

Newcastle Museum

Museum in Newcastle

Hours - 10am-5pm Tue-Sun, plus Mon school holidays

Contact - http://www.newcastlemuseum.com.au; 02-4974 1400

Location - 6 Workshop Way, Newcastle, Australia

This attractive museum in the restored Honeysuckle rail workshops tells a tale of the city from its Indigenous Awabakal origins to its rough-and-tumble social history, shaped by a cast of convicts, coal miners and steelworkers. Exhibitions are interactive and engaging, ranging from geology to local icons like Silverchair and the Newcastle Knights. If you're travelling with kids, check out hands-on science centre Supernova and the hourly sound-and-light show on the steelmaking process. There's also a cafe.

Fort Scratchley

Fort in Newcastle

Price - tunnel tour adult/child $12.50/6.50, full tour $16/8

Hours - 10am-4pm Wed-Mon, last tour 2.30pm

Contact - http://www.fortscratchley.com.au; 02-4974 5033

Location - Nobbys Rd, Newcastle, Australia

Perched above Newcastle Harbour, this intriguing military site was constructed during the Crimean War to protect the city against a feared Russian invasion. During WWII the fort returned fire on a Japanese submarine, making it the only Australian fort to have engaged in a maritime attack. It's free to enter, but the guided tours are worth taking, as you venture into the fort's labyrinth of underground tunnels. Head to the shop for tickets or for a self-guided-tour brochure.

Christ Church Cathedral

Cathedral in Newcastle

Hours - 7am-6pm

Contact -
http://www.newcastlecathedral.org.au; 02-
4929 2052

Location - 52 Church St, Newcastle,
Australia

Dominating the city skyline, Newcastle's Anglican cathedral (begun in 1892, finished in 1979 and re-finished in 1997 after heavy damage in the 1989 earthquake) is filled with treasures like a gold chalice and a remembrance book made from jewellery donated by locals who lost loved ones in WWI. The self-guided tour offers an insight into special features such as the fine pre-Raphaelite stained-glass window by Edward Burne-Jones and William Morris.

Canberra

Lately, Canberra has been staking a claim for the title of 'coolest little capital' – and we're not just talking winter temperatures. Where else could you chill out in with fresh ground coffee, before spotting kangaroos in the capital's reserves then taking in some of the nation's best culture?

While every other Australian city was settled before Federation in 1901, the youthful capital was first called Canberra in 1913 making it the only Australian city founded when the nation existed. It's not your colonial capital; it's an Australian invention conceived of by visionary American architect Walter Burley Griffin and his wife Marion Mahony Griffin. Before the constructed capital, the Ngambri and Ngunnawal were the among the indigenous peoples who owned the land with ties stretching back over 20,000 years. The name Canberra is based on the Ngunnawal word for meeting.

Today, the city boasts expansive open spaces, broad boulevards, aesthetics influenced by the 19th-century Arts and Crafts Movement, and a seamless alignment of built and natural elements. Recent designer precincts around the lake – New Acton, Kingston Foreshore and a work in progress boardwalk around to the Acton Peninsula – have added a cosmopolitan atmosphere at the city's heart. During parliamentary sitting weeks, the city buzzes with national politics. When not talking policy, the city's developing a reputation for its festivals – the legendary Floriade, National Folk Festival and the freshly minted Canberra Writers Festival.

Experiences in Canberra

National Gallery of Australia

Top choice gallery in Canberra

Price - costs vary for special exhibitions

Hours - 10am-5pm

Contact - http://www.nga.gov.au; 02-6240 6502

Location - Parkes Pl, Parkes, Canberra, Australia

The nation's extraordinary art collection is showcased in a suitably huge purpose-built gallery within the parliamentary precinct. Almost every big name you could think of from the world of Australian and international art, past and present, is represented. Famous works include one of Monet's Waterlilies, several of Sidney Nolan's Ned Kelly paintings, Salvador Dali's Lobster Telephone, an Andy Warhol Elvis print and a triptych by Francis Bacon.

Highlights include the extraordinary Aboriginal Memorial from Central Arnhem Land in the lobby, created for Australia's 1988 bicentenary. The work of 43 artists, this 'forest of souls' presents 200 hollow log coffins (one for every year of European settlement) and is part of an excellent collection of Aboriginal and Torres Strait Islander art. Most of the Australian art is on the 1st floor, alongside a fine collection of Asian and Pacific art.

Free guided tours are offered hourly from 10.30am to 2.30pm.

National Portrait Gallery

Top choice gallery in Canberra

Hours - 10am-5pm

Contact - http://www.portrait.gov.au; 02-6102 7000

Location - King Edward Tce, Parkes, Canberra, Australia

Occupying a flash new purpose-built building, this wonderful gallery tells the story of Australia through its faces – from wax cameos of Indigenous Australians to colonial portraits of the nation's founding families, to Howard Arkley's DayGlo portrait of musician Nick Cave. There is a good cafe for post-exhibition coffee and reflection.

Australian Parliament House

Top choice notable building in Canberra

Hours - 9am-5pm

Contact - http://www.aph.gov.au; 02-6277 5399

Location - Canberra, Australia

Opened in 1988, Australia's national parliament building is a graceful and deeply symbolic piece of architecture. The building itself is embedded in the Australian soil, covered with a turf roof and topped by a spindly but soaring 81m-high flagpole. The same detailed thought has been applied to the interior and there's plenty to see inside, whether the politicians are haranguing each other in the chambers or not.

After passing through airport-style security, visitors are free to explore large sections of the building and watch parliamentary proceedings from the public galleries. The only time that tickets are required is for the high theatre of Question Time in the House of Representatives (2pm on sitting days); tickets are free but must be booked through the Sergeant at Arms. See the website for a calendar of sitting days.

After entering through the Marble Foyer, pop into the Great Hall to take a look at the vast tapestry, which took 13 weavers two years to complete. Upstairs in the corridors surrounding the hall, there are interesting displays including temporary exhibits from the Parliamentary art collection. Look out for a 1297 edition of the Magna Carta and the original of Michael Nelson Tjakamarra's Possum & Wallaby Dreaming, which features both on the $5 note and writ large as the mosaic you passed in Parliament's forecourt.

There are further displays in the Members' Hall, ringed with august portraits of former prime ministers. From the hall, corridors branch off towards the two debating chambers. Australia has a Westminster-style democracy and its chambers echo the color scheme of the famous 'Mother of Parliaments' in London, with a subtle local twist. Rather than the bright red of the House of Lords and the deep green of the lower house, Australia's parliament house uses a dusky pink for its Senate and a muted green for the House of Representatives, inspired by the tones of the local eucalypts.

Lifts head up to the roof where there are lawns designed for people to walk on – a reminder to the politicians below that this is the 'people's house'. As the focal point of Canberra, this is the best place to get a perspective on Walter Burley Griffin's city design. Your eyes are drawn immediately along three axes, with the Australian War Memorial backed by Mt Ainslie directly ahead, the commercial centre on an angle to the left and Duntroon (representing the military) on an angle to the right. Interestingly, the church is denied a prominent place in this very 20th-century design.

Free guided tours (30 minutes on sitting days, 45 minutes on nonsitting days) depart at 9.30am, 11am, 1pm, 2pm and 3.30pm.

Australian War Memorial

Top choice museum in Canberra

Hours - 10am-5pm

Contact - http://www.awm.gov.au; 02-6243 4211

Location - Treloar Cres, Campbell, Canberra, Australia

Canberra's glorious art deco war memorial is a highlight in a city filled with interesting architecture. Built to commemorate 'the war to end all wars', it opened its doors in 1941 when the next world war was already in full swing. Attached to it is a large, exceptionally well designed museum devoted to the nation's military history.

The entrance opens onto a commemorative courtyard, which encloses a pool of remembrance where an eternal flame burns. The walls of the surrounding cloister are engraved with the names of Australia's war dead. A Last Post ceremony is held here every evening at 4.55pm, just before the doors are shut for the night. Behind the courtyard is the Byzantine-influenced Hall of Memory, a spectacular space topped with a dome and encrusted with mosaics and stained glass. Beneath the monumental statues representing servicewomen and the three branches of the military lies the Tomb of the Unknown Australian Soldier, representing all Australians who have given their lives during wartime.

The museum has halls dedicated to WWI, WWII and conflicts from 1945 to the present day, as well as a spectacular aircraft hall. Every 15 minutes a sound-and-light show is staged in either the massive Anzac Hall or the Vietnam Gallery, starting with Striking by Night, which re-creates a WWII night operation over Berlin (staged on the hour).

Free guided tours leave frequently from the main entrance's Orientation Gallery. Alternatively, purchase the self-guided tour leaflet ($5). There's also a free audio guide available for the WWI hall, where you can select from a range of themed tours.

Museum of Australian Democracy

Top choice museum in Canberra

Price - adult/child/family $2/1/5

Hours - 9am-5pm

Contact - http://www.moadoph.gov.au; 02-6270 8222

Location - Old Parliament House, 18 King George Tce, Parkes, Canberra, Australia

The seat of government from 1927 to 1988, this elegantly proportioned building offers visitors a taste of the political past. Displays cover Australian prime ministers, the roots of democracy and the history of local protest movements. You can also visit the old Senate and House of Representative chambers, the parliamentary library and the prime minister's office. Kids will love the Play Up area including dress ups and a play room based on the UN's Right to Shelter, while those with a thing for bling will enjoy the replica crown jewels.

National Museum of Australia

Top choice museum in Canberra

Price - tours adult/child $15/10

Hours - 9am-5pm

Contact - http://www.nma.gov.au; 02-6208 5000

Location - Lawson Cres, Acton Peninsula, Canberra, Australia

As well as telling Australia's national story, this museum hosts blockbuster touring exhibitions. The Gallery of First Australians is jam-packed with Aboriginal artefacts is a highlight. However, the disjointed layout of the displays means that the museum didn't quite gel in the way that Canberra's other national cultural institutions do.

Questacon

Museum in Canberra

Price - adult/child $23/18

Hours - 9am-5pm

Contact - http://www.questacon.edu.au; 02-6270 2800

Location - King Edward Tce, Parkes, Canberra, Australia

This kid-friendly science centre has educational and fun interactive exhibits. Explore the physics of sport, athletics and fun parks; cause tsunamis; and take shelter from cyclones and earthquakes. Exciting science shows, presentations and puppet shows are all included.

Australian National Botanic Gardens

Gardens in Canberra

Hours - 8.30am-5pm

Contact - http://www.nationalbotanicgardens.gov.au; 02-6250 9588

Location - Clunies Ross St, Acton, Canberra, Australia

On Black Mountain's lower slopes, these large gardens showcase Australian floral diversity over 35 hectares of cultivated garden and 50 hectares of remnant bushland. Various themed routes are marked out, with the best introduction being the 30-to-45 minute main path, which takes in the eucalypt lawn (70 species are represented), rock garden, rainforest gully and Sydney Region garden. A 3.2km bushland nature trail leads to the garden's higher reaches.

The visitor centre is the departure point for free hour-long guided walks at 11am and 2pm. If you'd prefer a more sedentary experience, an electric bus departs on the

Flora Explorer Tour (adult/child $6/3) at 10.30am and 1.30pm on weekends.

Cairns

Cairns (pronounced 'cans') has come a long way since its beginnings as a boggy swamp and rollicking goldfields port. Heaving under the weight of countless resorts, tour agencies, souvenir shops and a million reminders of its proximity to the Great Barrier Reef, Cairns is unabashedly geared towards tourism.

Old salts claim Cairns has lost its soul, but it does have an infectious holiday vibe. The city centre is more boardshorts than briefcases, and you'll find yourself throwing away all notions of speed and schedules here, thanks to heady humidity and a hearty hospitality that can turn a short stroll into an impromptu social event. Fittingly, Cairns is awash with bars, clubs, eateries and cafes suiting all budgets. There's no beach in town, but the magnificent Esplanade Lagoon more than makes up for it; otherwise, the northern beaches are but a local bus ride or short drive away.

Experiences in Cairns

Cairns Esplanade, Boardwalk & Lagoon

Waterfront in Cairns

Hours - lagoon 6am-9pm Thu-Tue, noon-9pm Wed

Contact - http://www.cairns.qld.gov.au/esplanade

Location - Cairns, Australia

Sunseekers and fun-lovers flock to Cairns Esplanade's spectacular swimming lagoon on the city's reclaimed foreshore. The artificial, sandy-edged, 4800-sq-metre saltwater pool is lifeguard patrolled and illuminated nightly. The adjacent 3km foreshore boardwalk has picnic areas, birdwatching vantage points, free barbecues and fitness equipment. Follow the signposts for the excellent Muddy's, which has playgrounds and water fun for little kids, and the skate ramp, beach volleyball courts, bouldering park and Fun Ship playground.

Markets, concerts, festivals and free fitness classes are regular occurrences on the Esplanade; check the website for happenings.

Flecker Botanic Gardens

Top choice gardens in Cairns

Hours - grounds 7.30am-5.30pm, visitor centre 9am-4.30pm Mon-Fri, 10am-2.30pm Sat & Sun

Contact - http://www.cairns.qld.gov.au/cbg; 07-4032 6650

Location - 64 Collins Ave, Cairns, Australia

These gorgeous gardens are an explosion of greenery and rainforest plants. Highlights include a section devoted to Aboriginal plant use, the Gondwana Heritage Garden, and an excellent conservatory filled with butterflies and exotic flowers. Staff at the made-of-mirrors visitor centre can advise on free guided garden walks (daily from 10am).

Follow the Rainforest Boardwalk to Saltwater Creek and Centenary Lakes, a birdwatcher's delight. Uphill from the gardens, Mt Whitfield Conservation Park has walking tracks through the rainforest to city viewpoints.

Rusty's Markets

Top choice market in Cairns

Hours - 5am-6pm Fri & Sat, to 3pm Sun

Contact - http://www.rustysmarkets.com.au; 07-4040 2705

Location - 57-89 Grafton St, Cairns, Australia

No weekend in Cairns is complete without a visit to this busy and vibrant multicultural market. Weave (and taste) your way through piles of seasonal tropical fruits, veggies and herbs, plus farm-fresh honey, locally grown flowers, excellent coffees, curries, cold drinks, antiques and more.

Cairns Regional Gallery

Gallery in Cairns

Price - adult/child $5/free

Hours - 9am-5pm Mon-Fri, 10am-5pm Sat, 10am-2pm Sun

Contact -
http://www.cairnsregionalgallery.com.au;
07-4046 4800

Location - cnr Abbott & Shields Sts, Cairns,
Australia

The permanent collection of this acclaimed
gallery, housed in the heritage-listed former
State Government Insurance Office (1936),
has an emphasis on local and Indigenous
work. It also hosts prominent visiting
exhibitions and workshops; at the very least,
have a gander at the excellent gift shop or a
coffee at the attached Perrotta's.

Uluru-Kata Tjuta National Park

National park in Uluru-Kata Tjuta National Park

Price - adult/child 3-day pass $25/free

Hours - sunrise-sunset

Contact - https://parksaustralia.gov.au/uluru/

Location - Uluru-Kata Tjuta National Park, Australia

Nothing can really prepare you for the immensity, grandeur, changing color and stillness of 'the rock'. It really is a sight that will sear itself onto your mind. The World Heritage–listed icon has attained the status of a pilgrimage. Uluru, the equally impressive Kata Tjuta (the Olgas) and the surrounding area are of deep cultural significance to the traditional owners, the Pitjantjatjara and Yankuntjatjara Aboriginal peoples (who refer to themselves as Anangu).

The Anangu officially own the national park, which is leased to Parks Australia and jointly administered.

There's plenty to see and do: meandering walks, bike rides, guided tours, desert culture and simply contemplating the many changing colours and moods of the great monolith itself.

The only accommodation is at the Ayers Rock Resort in the Yulara village, 20km from the Rock. Expect premium Prices, reflecting the remote locale.

The Daintree

The Daintree represents many things: Unesco World Heritage–listed rainforest, a river, a reef, laid-back villages and the home of its traditional custodians, the Kuku Yalanji people. It encompasses the coastal lowland area between the Daintree and Bloomfield Rivers, where the rainforest tumbles right down to the coast. It's a fragile, ancient ecosystem, once threatened by logging, but now protected as a national park.

Part of the Wet Tropics World Heritage Area, the spectacular region from the Daintree River north to Cape Tribulation features ancient rainforest, sandy beaches and rugged mountains. North of the Daintree River, electricity is supplied by generators or, increasingly, solar power. Shops and services are limited, and mobile-phone reception is patchy at best. The Daintree River Ferry carries wanderers and their wheels across the river every 15 minutes or so.

Experiences in The Daintree

Daintree Discovery Centre

Top choice nature reserve in Cow Bay & Around

Price - adult/child/family $32/16/78

Hours - 8.30am-5pm

Contact - http://www.discoverthedaintree.com; 07-4098 9171

Location - Tulip Oak Rd, Cow Bay & Around, Australia

This award-winning attraction's aerial walkway, which includes a 23m tower used to study carbon levels, takes you high into the forest canopy. A theatre screens films on cassowaries, crocodiles, conservation and climate change. An excellent audio-guide tour and interpretive booklet is included in the admission fee; tickets are valid for reentry for seven days.

Daintree Rainforest

Forest in The Daintree

Contact - http://www.daintreerainforest.com

Location - The Daintree, Australia

The Daintree is the accessible section of breathtakingly beautiful coastal lowland rainforest in the Wet Tropics World Heritage Area. This dense, lush region hosts amazing pockets of biodiversity with unique swamp and mangrove forest habitats, eucalypt woodlands, native birds and tropical rainforest.

Myall Beach

Beach in Cape Tribulation

Location - Cape Tribulation, Australia

Easy access from the village makes this Cape Trib's most popular beach for strolling. Areas of fringing reef on Myall Beach are exposed at low tide, allowing swimmers to explore the rock pools. It's best reached via the Dubuji Boardwalk and car park. At the southernmost end, you can explore the Myall Creek mouth.

At the northern point of the beach you can climb out onto the Cape Trib headland. Don't try and go around it – vertical cliffs make this impossible. Halfway to the headland is Mason Creek: check out the sheltered nook in the mangroves, a popular spot for birdwatching.

Cape Tribulation Beach

Beach in Cape Tribulation

Location - Cape Tribulation, Australia

North of the headland, Cape Tribulation
Beach is a lovely crescent of often empty
sand. Easiest access is via the Kulki
Boardwalk and car park at the southern end.

Walu Wugirriga Lookout

Viewpoint in Cow Bay & Around

Location - Cow Bay & Around, Australia

Coming to or from the ferry, stop in at this lookout high in the Alexandra Range for rainforest and coastal views.

Bat House

Wildlife reserve in Cape Tribulation

Price - $5

Hours - 10.30am-3.30pm Tue-Sun

Contact - http://www.austrop.org.au; 07-4098 0063

Location - Cape Tribulation Rd, Cape Tribulation, Australia

A nursery for injured or orphaned fruit bats (flying foxes), run by conservation organisation Austrop.

Conclusion

Thank you for purchasing this Australia travel guide book, I hope it was of use to you. If you are looking for more travel guides, please visit my Amazon Author page.

Printed in Great Britain
by Amazon

74747777R00156